Padre Pio
OF PIETRELCINA

"My Jesus, save everyone; I offer myself as victim for them all. Strengthen me, take my heart, fill it with your love, and then command whatever you will".

Padre Pio of Pietrelcina

Padre Pio is a book prepared for publication by the Franciscans of the Immaculate [marymediatrix.com], POB 3003, New Bedford, MA, 02741-3003- Translator: Fr. Alphonsus Mary Sutton, FI

Imprimatur   ✠ Most. Rev. Sean Patrick O'Malley
                OFM Cap., Bishop of Fall River
                Massachussets, USA
                March 25, 1999
                Solemnity of the Annunciation

The Imprimatur is a declaration of the Roman Catholic Church that the work is free from error in matters of faith and morals; but in no way does it imply that she endorses the contents of the work.

Padre Pio

OF PIETRELCINA

Fr. Stefano M. Manelli

Franciscans of the Immaculate
New Bedford, MA 1999

Preface

As we go through the very rich, but long and detailed biographies of Padre Pio of Pietrelcina[1], we wonder about the reaction of many people, especially the young, who want to read about this man. How can we expect all people to read through books that are long?

On the other hand, the desire to know at least the more essential and characteristic things in the extraordinary life of Padre Pio, needs to be satisfied. This would benefit everybody, especially our youth, to whom we must offer lofty and challenging models.

We offer here an early attempt at such a biography. It is but a modest profile of this son of St. Francis, this twentieth century spiritual father of an immense multitude.

Where is the value of knowing about Padre Pio? We find it in the truth that God sends Saints that meet the needs of the times. Every Saint is a prophet for his times. And every prophet is a beacon casting light upon the present and future pathway of men.

In the Gospel we read that Jesus grieved over Jerusalem because that city, instead of welcoming and heeding the prophets, had persecuted them and slain them, thus drawing punishment and disaster upon herself (cf. Mt. 23:37).

We, too, have our prophets—yes, true ones sent by God, who have labored and taught after Jesus' example. It is our duty to know them and follow them in order not to earn the reproof of our Lord.

One of these prophets certainly is Padre Pio. We do not hesitate to call him a prophet extraordinary in holiness and works, worthy to stand alongside the greatest prophets of the Church.

He speaks to the men of today, so needful of God. He points out to all, the way in the Gospel to holiness and to the perfect following of Christ Our Lord.

Fr. Stefano M. Manelli, FI, STD

Table of Contents

WHO IS PADRE PIO?

"I will cherish Pietrelcina."

Pietrelcina is a small town in the Province of Benevento in central Italy. It is situated in the hills of the southern borderlands of Sannio. It is rustic, charming and impressive in its littleness and poverty. On one hill in the town a cluster of poor homes are castled together. It is the zone called Castello. During the Middle Ages a small castle was constructed there. It was on a rocky eminence known as the Morgia, or Morgione about which memories and legends have clustered down the centuries.

The old parish church of Pietrelcina is built on the highest point of the Morgia. Today it is called the Church of St. Ann. Before it a panoramic terrace descends abruptly toward a creek below called the Pantanella.

The area known as Castello is dearest to the citizens of Pietrelcina. It is as it were the cornerstone of the town, today even more cherished because of the birth of Padre Pio. Not rarely at San Giovanni Rotondo was Padre Pio heard to remark to visitors about to return to Pietrelcina:

"Say hello to the Morgia for me."

1

Perhaps the simple, loveable people of that time have disappeared for good.

The most distinctive feature of the Castello district is its rural beauty jumping live from the narrow, twisting lanes, rising, descending, circling, almost aimlessly, crossing to form lovely, quiet angles, where usually some old lady from a door window would be observing every passerby.

Pietrelcina spread out through the small sorrounding valleys, extending to the towns of Piana Romana, San Nicola, Barrata, Difesa, Monte, Valluni— so forming a landscape rich in color and pleasing to the eye.

The Madonna della Libera

Pietrelcina is a healthy, hard-working community. Customs and behavior standards are preserved with an enduring zeal for local tradition. The people are warm-hearted. They like music and are fond of religious celebrations on days of special devotion and local interest, specially on the feast day of their patron, the lovely Madonna della Libera, whose shrine is linked with the miraculous.

Pietrelcina had about three thousand inhabitants when Padre Pio was born in 1887, and given the name Francis. Today the town has a few more inhabitants.

But a future awaits it because of the glorious role played by this remarkable native son.

One day Padre Pio uttered these words: "During my life I have cherished San Giovanni Rotondo. After my death I will cherish and favor Pietrelcina."

Was this, too, a prophecy? Indeed, beyond doubt. For at this very moment projects are being planned and executed to upgrade the birthplace of Padre Pio. New roads, houses, the development of Piana Romana, so rich in important events and memories, cultural activities, the increase of piety and the formation of so many Church and secular groups already are engaging the efforts of the responsible ecclesiastical and civil authorities to meet the needs of an ever increasing number of pilgrims and visitors desirous of knowing their village of the Sannio blessed by the birth and presence of Padre Pio.

His parents

The parents of a saint are nearly always persons distinguished by goodness and virtue. They are the precious root of a plant still more precious. Remember for example, the parents of St. Thèrése and of St. Pius X. So too the parents of Padre Pio of Pietrelcina. They will pass into history not only for the merits of their great, stigmatized son, but by reason of their great goodness and piety as well.

Grazio Forgione and Maria Giuseppa di Nunzio were the happy parents of Padre Pio. They were married in 1881. Youthful, upright and sober-minded, they came from families of modest means. They owned a bit of farmland that was barely enough for them to squeeze out what they needed to live on, for better or worse.

Every morning before sunrise Grazio used to get on his donkey and set out for the countryside to work his land, leading a young goat to pasture. And later on Francis, the little shepherd attentive to the lambs to feed would lead them behind him. He labored hard the year round. His working hours ended in the evening toward sundown, when he nearly always brought home some fruit from the fields for the family table.

Maria Giuseppa, or Mamma Peppa, as people often called her, was a kind-hearted, industrious housewife. She saw to it that her husband and her children were adequately provided for. She would rise at night to make bread and cheese. Several times a day she went to fetch water from the Madunnella, a nearby spring, where there was a little wayside shrine with an image of the Queen of heaven and on either side images of St. Michael and St. Anthony. The journey was short but tiresome, for she had to return carrying her load of water up some twenty uneven steps.

If there was but little of everything in their home, Maria Giuseppa knew how to manage its distribution wisely. She prepared what was needed for each day and saved up things for feast days.

At Christmas there were the characteristic "zeppole" which the children ate in great quantity with that avid and genuine appetite proper to the little ones. For Easter there were sweets with bread made of whitest flour, rice pizza with ricotta and the "tortano", a kind of cake with an egg at the center.

Every year Maria Giuseppa gave some of their farm products as an offering for the novena for the Poor Souls in Purgatory. She was generous, too, in giving the firstfruits of their harvest to the poorer families.

Here we have a couple conspicuous for their uprightness and sobriety, who dedicated themselves to bringing up a truly Christian family—one of those that "fear the Lord and walk in His ways" (Ps. 127:1).

The homestead

A typical road in the Castello district is the Vico Storto Valle. It is a long lane, narrow and bending. In some places there are gray, rocky walls alongside it, and it is surfaced in stone. Doors of dark, heavy wood are here and there on either side. This is the street on which Grazio and Maria Giuseppa made their home.

They lived in a rambling dwelling. In one end was the kitchen joined to a makeshift dining room that served as a bedroom for the children. In a court in front there was a stall for the donkey and a woodpile. A step away from the kitchen a door entered into the couple's bedroom. A few yards further on one mounted a steep stone stairway up a rocky eminence, the Morgione, to reach a solitary room called the tower room (torretta). Padre Pio had that room a long time during his stay at Pietrelcina as a young religious on sick leave. He liked the location for its solitude and silence. It reminds one, even now, of an eagle's nest.

Visitors today find these places much the same together with the district of Piana Romana. The attractive rustic simplicity that is noticed in these frugal surroundings is something that can uplift one. There is an absence of luxury, of superfluity, of the thousand and one unnecessary items that fill our homes. Possessions are reduced to what is essential. "Blessed are the poor in spirit, for theirs is the kingdom of heaven" (Matt. 5:1).

In this house Padre Pio was born, the second of five that lived to adulthood—two boys and three girls, whose names were Michael, Francis, Felicita, Pellegrina, and Grazia. Three others died at an early age: Francis, who died a few days after birth; Amalia, who died not quite two years old; Mario, who died at eleven months. Thus Mamma Peppa gave birth to eight children. In the ways of God she was fruitful. She and Grazio her husband knew that, as holy Scripture declares, "The inheritance of the

Lord are children: the reward, the fruit of the womb" (Ps. 126:3). And throughout his life Padre Pio had a special preference and blessing for every numerous family that lived according to the will of God. And among the many, many large families directed spiritually by him, there was one especially beloved, perhaps the largest, a family of 21 children, the Manelli family (to which the present writer belongs). Newly married Settimio and Licia Manelli entrusted to Padre Pio their family. He accepted saying: *"This is my family".*

"He was a beautiful baby"

Padre Pio was born on Wednesday, May 25, 1887. The first whimpers of this little creature were heard in the Forgione homestead at about five in the evening while bells were pealing their summons to the faithful to come to church and honor the Blessed Virgin during her beautiful month. He was baptized the next day in the old parish church of Pietrelcina, which had been dedicated to St. Mary of the Angels, and he was named Francis.

One cannot help but admire the care taken by these parents to have their child baptized as soon as possible so as to free him of original sin and fill him with the grace of God. Great must have been the sacrifice of the mother bedridden and so unable to be present at the Baptism in Church. But for her, a christian rich in wisdom, it was far more important the child should at once be no longer a "child of wrath" (Eph 2, 3), but one reborn of God, a new christian, a small "temple of God" (I Cor 3, 16) bearing the name of St. Francis, the seraph of Assisi.

There is a happy coincidence about the name given to this child and the name of the parish church, St. Mary of the Angels. For it is well known how St. Francis of Assisi was associated with the little church of the Portiuncula bearing that name on the verdant plain of Umbria. Later on, when this child was to learn about the Saint of Assisi, after whom he was named, this knowledge would influence his choice of vocation.

The parents acted wisely. It is no small matter to have the child baptized as soon as possible and to give to each child baptized the name of a Saint. Surely the child will eventually find in that Saint whose name he bears a heavenly protector and model for life, particularly potent when the name is that of a Saint as stupendous as Francis of Assisi.

Meantime he developed quickly into a very beautiful infant. His cousin, Grazia Forgione, testified, "He was very pretty. His face was beautiful. He was completely healthy and clear-skinned. He was beautiful in every way."

"He will be honored all over the world."

Pietrelcina like so many towns of the Sannio had its town astrologer. His name was Giuseppe Fajella, a close neighbor to the Forgiones. His reputed skill was based on his familiarity with the so-called *Rutilio,* a book which explained the signs of the Zodiac and horoscopes according to the wisdom of ancient astrologers. It was hard for mothers not to yield to a natural, perhaps naïve, curiosity about the future of their children. So Mamma Peppa chose to take her baby boy to the man.

She wrapped her child in a warm shawl and carried him to Fajella's home. The man consulted his Rutilio. Then, in an effort to speak slowly, he stammered out his surprising prediction: *"This child will be honored by the whole world. Much money will pass through his hands, but he will never possess anything. He will die at an advanced age."*

In later years when Mamma Peppa would narrate this, she would speak of the astonishment she felt and would tell what thoughts then passed in her mind: "Who knows? Maybe when he grows up Francis will go to America and make a fortune and become famous..."

We may be sure she did not forget the prediction, and that she had joy in seeing it come true in a beautiful, extraordinary way. Similar episodes are told in the lives of various great Saints. They may seem legendary to many, but God knows how to use even means like these to show forth His glory.

A mysterious, elderly pilgrim came to the home of St. Francis of Assisi when he was newly born and predicted to his mother that her child was to be "among the best men of the world."

He wept behind the door

Meantime the child was growing into a handsome, healthy, good boy. At first his crying and screaming tried his father's patience when he had come home weary and could not sleep in peace at night.

"Doesn't this baby ever run out of breath?"
Grazio lamented when he could stand no more. One time when Mamma Peppa was away the child started wailing as though he were being strangled. His father, after trying his best to pacify him by holding him in his arms, lost patience and cast him on the bed, muttering angrily, "It is the devil who has been born in my home!" When Padre Pio used to tell of this, he always ended by saying, "From that day on I did not cry any more."

One can truthfully say that he became from then on a good, quiet child, breathing the pure air of a simple and fruitfully pious family life that was deeply religious. Both parents attached great importance to the task of implanting in their children an appreciation of God and of religion. Every evening the family recited the Rosary together. This prayer held a place of honor. Other things might be sacrificed in that home, but not the Rosary.

In his own way little Francis began early to show an uncommon appreciation of religion. His mother has left us a meaningful detail about this. When Francis was about five years old he happened to hear a blasphemy. He then hid behind the door and wept. His innocent soul felt the wound of seeing God insulted.

One time when he was a little older he passed by the home of a shoemaker, with whom he used to stop and talk; for they were on familiar terms. The day was Sunday, and he saw the man's daughter toiling away with her needlework, sewing a band on a dress.

"Andianella, today we don't work. It's Sunday."

Showing her annoyance, the girl answered, "Little boy, you are too small to talk like that."

Francis went away. A little later he returned with a pair of scissors. He grabbed the band she had been sewing and cut it into pieces. The girl cried out in protest, but Francis was quite tranquil.

Not that he would have behaved this way when older, but from that time on Francis showed an uncompromising attitude toward evil. This was to mark his behavior for the fifty years or so of his apostolate in the confessional. God must come before all other considerations.

"I want to go to church"

Other more hidden events distinguished the soul of this child, even from the age of five. He was not only very sensitive about matters pertaining to God, but he began having visions of spirits, at times very beautiful ones, and at times very ugly ones.

The child was in no position to appreciate the extraordinary character of these phenomena and did not know about the real character of ecstasies, raptures and diabolical interventions. He did not speak of them to anyone and considered such events to be the ordinary thing in everybody's life. He was disinclined to think himself to be a privileged person. He was well aware that life has to do with two realms of opposing realities; and these are, on the one hand, the reality of God and of heaven, and on the other hand the reality of the devil and of things that are sinful. He committed himself entirely to God's side, and it was remarkable how he clung to the Church that spoke to him of God, that gave him God, that united him to God. The words "Voglio i' a la chiesa"—"I want to go to church, I want to be in and with the Church"—express Francis' determined will, a will stronger than his years.

His sister Grazia tells us that one evening when the church bell was sounding, Francis went at once to his grandmother and said, "I want to go to church!" There were others present who remarked, "But you have not

The Publisher acknowledges the use of selected texts and letters from:
Ita Ford, M.M. Letters. *Same Fate as the Poor* Collection. Maryknoll Sisters
Archives. Maryknoll Mission Archives. Maryknoll, New York. Used by permission of the Maryknoll Sisters of St. Dominic, Inc., Maryknoll, N.Y. All rights
reserved.

Transcriptions of selected texts and letters of Ita Ford by Phyllis Zagano.

Cover design by Cindy Dunne.

Cover photo courtesy of William P. Ford.

Library of Congress Cataloging-in-Publication Data

Zagano, Phyllis.
   Ita Ford : missionary martyr / Phyllis Zagano.
     p. cm.
   ISBN 0-8091-3663-5 (alk. paper)
   1. Ford, Ita, d. 1980. 2. Maryknoll Sisters—Latin America—Biography.
3. Missionaries—Latin America—Biography.   4. Christian martyrs—El
Salvador—Biography. I. Title.
BV2300.M4Z34   1996
266'.2'092—dc20
[B]
                                           96-5523
                                             CIP

Published by Paulist Press
997 Macarthur Boulevard
Mahwah, New Jersey 07430

Printed and bound in the
United States of America

ITA FORD
MISSIONARY MARTYR

PHYLLIS ZAGANO

PAULIST PRESS
New York / Mahwah, N.J.

had supper yet." Francis answered, "Who wants to think about supper? I must go to church with Grandmother."

Francis was assiduous and devout about attending church. He missed none of the parish functions. Each Sunday afternoon he attended catechism. He learned the hymns and attentively followed the pastor's religious instructions. At the age of ten he made his first Holy Communion, and he was confirmed when he was twelve. He learned early how to serve Mass, and served with a devotion that drew attention from the mothers who used to watch him during the holy Sacrifice. He looked as recollected and pretty as an angel as he knelt with his little hands devoutly joined at the foot of the altar.

If Francis' recollectedness did not make him a bit aloof to his playmates, it did keep him reserved and well-mannered in his associations and during the games that the children played. Ordinarily they played them in the yard in front of the church. Francis never "let himself go" when it came to play. He commonly limited himself to watching his friends play, or he preferred to play alone, according to his mother's testimony. Why? One answer is this: Because at times his companions broke out into bad language. This made him suffer. He loved decency, even in play.

A miracle before his eyes

One of the Saints most loved by the people of Pietrelcina was St. Pellegrino[2]. Just as St. Nicholas is a favorite at Bari and Saints Cosmas and Damian at Benevento, likewise St. Pellegrino drew many clients to his shrine at Altavilla Irpina.

One year his father, Grazio, took Francis to St. Pellegrino's shrine. The church was crowded with pilgrims from many different places. Francis went to a front pew to pray, where he became impressed at the sight of a poor woman carrying a deformed baby. The poor mother kept her eyes fixed on the Saint's image, as she sighed and prayed, "Heal my son! Heal my son!" Francis understood the child's unfortunate condition and the mother's grief. He was deeply moved and sympathetically added his own prayers to those of the unhappy mother.

A little time passed in this way, until Francis felt someone tugging him. "Francis, let us go," his father said.

"Another minute, please. Do wait a little longer, Papà." Meantime the woman kept on appealing with greater fervor for her son's cure. At a certain point, seeing she was not getting anywhere, she picked up her poor baby and put him onto the Saint's altar, crying, "If you don't want to cure him, take him! I don't want him!"

As soon as the infant landed on the altar, he got on his feet and standing quite erect, cried, "Mamma! Mamma!" A miracle had happened! The mother took her child and pressed him to her bosom.Meantime there was excitement all around her. Word quickly spread, even outside. A thick crowd gathered within the shrine.

When the parish priest learned of the miracle, he sounded the bell of thanksgiving, as was customary when the Saint bestowed a favor. Francis, more deeply impressed than ever and bewildered at what had happened before his eyes, appeared like someone petrified. Another stronger tug from his father induced him to move.

But it was too late. The dense throng compelled father and son to wait until it thinned out. After they had left, Francis' father rebuked him. But he would never forget the miracle that happened before his gaze, which profoundly convinced him of the power of prayer and of the intercession of the Saints.

Studious little shepherd

As soon as the boys in the Forgione home grew big enough to be of help, they were assigned their chores. When Francis became able to take their three or four sheep with their nanny goat out to pasture, he became

the family's shepherd. Each morning one would see this handsome little shepherd setting out with his little flock toward Piana Romana. Most of the time he went alone. But sometimes he was joined by another little shepherd of the town. It was apt to be his cousin, Mercurio, who took along seven or eight sheep.

The two boys used to have their fun and reveal their very different temperaments. Mercurio was high-spirited and ever inclined to jokes and pranks, and might even have a tussle. We know that boys like to wrestle with each other in a way that no one hardly ever gets hurt. But Francis did not like that kind of fun, and if ever he got into a tussle, he was sure to regret it.

Once he managed to get the better of his companion and pinned him down. His companion broke out with bad words. At once Francis released him and, grief-stricken, hastened away.

Francis' preference was for a game that involved marching. With care and enthusiasm he would get it started and it would last a long time. His cousin Mercurio, as an old man, used to repeat, "We were ever doing the processions."

Francis was more than just a shepherd. He was also a student. He was trying all by himself to learn to read. This was noteworthy, if one reflects that most of the old people in town were illiterate. Along the banks of the Castello creek there was a little schoolhouse where

the most elementary instruction was given. There little children learned to read, and the brighter ones also learned to write. The schoolmaster was a hemp-worker. For his instructions he was happy to receive a half-lira a month. Every evening he assembled little shepherds and other young peasants and held school.

Francis was among the most attentive and diligent of his little group. He used to take his books with him out to the pastures to study. At noon he used to eat his lunch. Unlike the others, he would do it with the manners of a gentleman. He had his bread in a clean napkin. Before eating he would spread a little tablecloth over his knees. If a little food fell, he picked it up so that it would not go to waste.

Right after his meal he studied. Then his companions, who did not want to study, used to tease him in a hundred ways. They would shove him, throw sand or leaves onto his book, or snatch away his cap, in order to get him to leave his studies and come play with them.

Saved by fried peppers

Typhus is a dangerous and much-dreaded disease. People stricken with it in those days did not easily escape death. Francis was stricken with it. The manner in which he recovered was something quite unusual. His fever was high, he was more dead than alive, and

had only a number of hours more to live. He overheard the doctor tell this fact to his mother, who began to quietly weep.

It was harvest time. The farmers on the Piana Romana were busy at work. In spite of her grief, Mamma Giuseppa had to prepare lunch for the harvesters. She made an ample platter of fried peppers, the kind that are hot and strong. But the harvesters only ate part of them. More than half were left over, and Mamma Giuseppa put them away in a cupboard.

They gave off an appetizing scent that appealed to Francis. While he had seemed to have no appetite, he was very fond of fried peppers. As soon as he was left alone in the room, he got out of bed. As he could not stand on his feet, he crawled on his hands and knees to the cupboard, opened it, and ate all the peppers that were left over.

When he was back in bed, he felt a burning thirst. He called his brother Michael and asked for a drink. His brother brought a bottle of milk and served him some in a spoon, as they had been doing. But Francis took hold of the bottle and began to drink from it, to his brother's surprise.

When their mother later came to look for the peppers, she found the platter empty and could not understand how they had disappeared. She did not even suspect that Francis was responsible. She inquired, but

nobody would admit their guilt. The empty platter remained a mystery. Meantime the effects of Francis' feast were against all rules. It could have been fatal, but it produced a radical change for the better, curing Francis of the typhus and restoring his health. Once he had recovered, Francis explained to his family the mystery of the fried peppers.

THE PIOUS LITTLE BROTHER

I want to be a religious

One day Francis was in church and heard a sermon on St. Michael the Archangel. The preacher was Don Giuseppe Orlando, a young priest and a Pietrelcinian. Some years later, after ordination, Padre Pio met Don Giuseppe and told him, *"If I am a priest, I owe it to you. I felt my vocation while I was listening to your sermon on St. Michael."* When he heard the sermon, Francis was about ten years old. On that occasion he was aware of a clear, strong call from God. He said nothing to his family at the time. Later on, in the year 1898, a young man from Pietrelcina, Rudolph Masone, had entered the Capuchin friary at Morcone. That year, for the first time, a Capuchin friar came to Pietrelcina to seek alms and collect donations of wheat from people of the region. He was a guest of the Masone family. He was known as Friar Camillo. He had a handsome beard, a satchel strapped over his back, and proved likable to everybody. He visited the Piana Romana area of the town, and Mamma Giuseppa gave him a generous supply of wheat. After a few friendly words and an assurance of his prayers, the friar cheerfully departed.

Francis had been present at the scene, looking fixedly at the good friar. He did not turn his eyes away until the man left the house.

Then, turning to Grazio, he said,

"Father!"

"What do you want, son?"

"I want to be a religious."

His mother, standing near, quickly broke in, "Become one of the friars of Paduli, so that we will always get to see you."

There was a monastery of Franciscan Friars Minor at Paduli, a town near Pietrelcina.

"No," Francis answered, *"I want to be a religious with a beard."*

Finally his father spoke, "Yes indeed! If you do your school work well, you will become a friar."

From that day onward the Forgione family began to talk more and more about Francis' Franciscan vocation. Bit by bit things became geared in this direction, things that required decisions of great importance for the family.

Grazio goes to America

Even during his later years Padre Pio would become deeply moved when he would say, "My father crossed the ocean twice in order to give me the chance to be-

come a friar." To enter the Capuchin novitiate it was necessary to have finished the ginnasio, which was equivalent to the American high school.

When the time approached for Francis to enter a ginnasio, Grazio[3] realized that the family's income, which depended on the fluctuations of the market and his harvests, would be too uncertain to enable him to promise the required monthly payments. He then made a generous and courageous decision. To make sure of the necessary income, he would go to work in America. What noble things is a father's heart not capable of?

He set out for the United States. He easily found work there on a farm. Proving himself industrious and conscientious, he was well-liked, and became the foreman of some farm-hands.

He kept his family informed and sent them money periodically. In spite of the distance, he was always concerned about Pietrelcina, his farmlands, and his family, and wanted to be well posted about them.

The one who kept up the correspondence with Grazio was Francis. In this task the boy showed care and devotion. He would tell his father whatever Grazio wanted to know and any important local news. His letters gave news about his mother, his brother and his sisters, and included their greetings and his fond hope that his father would return "safe and sound;" and Francis assured him of his "continuous prayers to our beautiful Virgin."

Conscientious and affectionate, Francis showed himself also deeply respectful and thoughtful in his letters. He addressed his father with the respectful "voi," and signed the letters as "Your obedient son," and at the end he would ask his father's blessing.

Gratitude for his father's great sacrifice, filial devotion to a father so generous, a feeling of indebtedness and respect toward one who had given him his life, a spirit of faith, of humility, and of submission to a father on earth who stood as the image and representative of the heavenly Father—all these sentiments were Francis', and he showed them. He gave a beautiful example of respectful Christian conduct in the relations between a son and his father.

Changing teachers

Francis was sent to Dominic Tizzano to begin his ginnasio, or high school studies.

Contrary to expectation, Francis was not successful in his schoolwork. He got nowhere and was unresponsive. When Giuseppa asked for a report, Tizzano gave his opinion in an abrupt, definitive reply, "Your son is a dummy. Send him out to take care of the sheep."

This was a bewildering disappointment to the poor mother. Francis was so docile and careful about everything. What could be the trouble?

The mystery was eventually solved. Libera Venturelli, a lady friendly with the Forgione family, declared that Francis was not at all happy to go to school to Tizzano because Tizzano had once been a priest and was now living with a woman. This greatly distressed Francis and was a hindrance to his schoolwork.

By the grace of God his mother was inspired to change him to another teacher, namely, Angelo Caccavo, a well respected schoolmaster in the town.

The change at once had good results. Francis made rapid progress. It was not hard to see why, when he proved to be an excellent student, well adjusted, diligent, esteemed by his teacher and fellow pupils.

The place where he usually did his studying was a tower room (or toretta). It was hard for anyone to bother him while he was up there. When he used to go out into the country to help with the farm work, at intervals he would go off to himself under a tree to study.

It was not infrequent that he had to go directly from the farmland in Piana Romana to the school in town. On the journey he would have to bear the sun and the rain. There are many testimonies of witnesses who used to see Francis on his way to school, anxious to be on time as he passed through the streets of the town with his books under his arm, modest and recollected. He counted punctuality as something important.

Once a lady, who was a friend of the Forgione family, saw Francis passing by her home and called, "Francis! Francis! Come here!"

Without stopping, the boy answered, "I have to go to school!" When the lady met his mother she could not resist complimenting him: "Your son certainly is a fine boy. He puts my son to shame."

Potatoes, vegetables, study

It often happened that Francis had to stay home alone while the rest of the family were out in the country. He would then prepare his own lunch and afterwards go back to his studies. It took very little to satisfy him. He never complained and was always happily tranquil home from school.

A neighbor, Virginia Fajella, reports that Francis once passed her house when returning home from school and greeted her. She returned the greeting and asked, "Have you now just come from school?"

"Yes."

"And now, what are you going to do about lunch?"

"Oh, I make something for myself to eat. Mother left some vegetables for me. So I will cook them today."

After he had eaten, he passed the same neighbor on his way to the tower room and greeted her again.

"Goodby, Virginia!"
"Goodby! Now you are going to study, I see."
"Yes. See you tomorrow."

This is the way he spent most of his high school days—at home, at school, in church, with regularity and perseverance, showing exactness and constancy.

We could certainly never say that it is the usual thing to find such seriousness and conscientiousness in a boy not yet fifteen. One is especially surprised to find this together with the virtues of kindness and thoughtfulness that he practiced. Francis showed a delicate conscience, a sense of duty, a serious manner, which all expressed an uncommon maturity in his outlook.

And so he is an example for the youngest, a model for the adolescent, ordinarily so restless, an example of dedication and fidelity for students, a model for children called to be ever respectful and loving toward their parents.

Francis still teaches this to everyone today, and he will always teach it in support of all those young boys and girls who desire to save themselves from "this world of darkness" (Eph 6,12), living "according to the Spirit" and not "according to the flesh (Rom 8,8) guarding their purity of heart and body, aspiring to things noble and grand, to thing eternal and divine, to the "things above" (Col 3,1)

Victim of pranks

We all know that many boys get an itch to provoke a humiliating situation for a companion, especially if he is exemplary and well respected. Once some companions of Francis decided to play a prank that would get him in trouble. They wrote a love letter, signing it "Francis Forgione," and saw to it that it reached one of the girls in the school. The girl was shocked and took it at once to the schoolmaster.

The schoolmaster was stunned, too; for he did not expected anything like this from his best pupil. He kept Francis in after school and showed him the letter bearing his signature. Then, without waiting for a reply, he gave him a good whipping.

"You bad boy! What a liberty for you to take!"

Poor Francis had no time to say a word of explanation or of self-defense. He could only protest, "It is not true! It is not true!" while he sought to dodge the strokes.

When the schoolmaster, Caccavo, learned the whole truth, he could not conceal his grief. His admiration increased for this good, patient boy, who desired no retaliation against the pranksters. Those boys had wanted to provoke a little scandal over Francis because they realized the great difference between his behavior and theirs, especially in associating with girls.

While some boys like to play jokes and tricks on girls, Francis kept himself completely above reproach everywhere—at school, in church, on the street. It had become second nature with him, when girls were around, to control his eyes modestly, to keep his head a bit inclined, and to avoid becoming too familiar with any of them. And so it was not he that looked at girls, but the girls would turn their heads about to note the beauty that shone especially in his eyes.

After many years his former female acquaintances testified that they had used to provoke Francis' attention because they felt attracted by his good looks and seriousness. One went so far as to slip a note into his pocket expressing her affection. But Francis cared nothing about such things. He was unfamiliar with these ways of girls and wanted to stay unfamiliar. This explains how he kept his virginal purity throughout his life.

Shortly before he left to go to the Capuchins, another trick was played on him. A schoolmate passed the word that he was courting the daughter of the local railroad agent. The word reached the pastor, an archpriest, who took drastic measures, excluding Francis from his group of clerics and forbidding him to serve Mass or any other function.

Francis did not know what it was all about, and for a month he found the archpriest harsh and stern, without knowing why. Fortunately the priest investigated,

and the truth about the trick came to light. Then he told Francis why he had dealt so sternly. He put him back among his altar boys, and to make up for what Francis had suffered, he would not accept the customary compensation for preparing all the documents Francis needed for entering the religious life.

"Two forces were tearing my heart"

Meanwhile the day was approaching when Francis would become a Capuchin novice at the Morcone friary near Benevento. Within his soul Francis was experiencing alternating times of light and of painful darkness. If this youth had always been careful and thoughtful, even in small matters, he felt he had to proceed with much seriousness and thoughtfulness during a time on which his whole future depended. Later on he was to reveal the story about his final decisions that he made before entering the novitiate.

"Two forces were tearing my heart," he was to admit. What were they? One was his love for God, to whom he wished to give himself completely. The other was a love for creatures, which were luring him with persuasive tricks. The struggle was neither brief nor painless. Francis knew how limited and inferior creatures are. He understood their short duration and their delusiveness. But fallen nature would not stop pressing its

claims to have a life of fun, and so protested against the observant religious life that meant self-denial and the sacrifice of all self-seeking. The nature of the struggle was quite clear to him. It was between a religious vocation and the attractions of this world. Francis realized that he could not gain anything by treating the matter lightly. He feared that creatural attractions would be able to triumph in the course of time over his spirit, as often happens to souls, and would choke the good seed, that is, the calling from God.

With the aid of prayer and earnest meditation, Francis was able to reach a lasting interior peace. He later said that he gained this victory from the strength God gave him "to forsake the world and its path to ruin and dedicate himself entirely to serving God." This happy outcome received a confirmation in an extraordinary vision that God granted him during a meditation. During the vision he saw a man who looked very majestic and beautiful, who took him by the hand and led him to a battlefield where there were two opposing armies. One was composed of angels and the other of devils. Between the two armies there was a monster so huge that he seemed like a mountain. Francis perceived that he, Francis, was being directed by his guide who held his hand, to enter into combat with this ugly monster.

He drew back at first, full of terror. But then, relying on the help of his guide, he entered the combat. It

was a terrible conflict, but finally Francis won, and the monster with his army of devils gave up and fled while the angels rejoiced.

Then Francis' guide placed a bright crown on his head and told him, "I am saving another crown that is more beautiful, which is for you if you know how to keep fighting always against the one whom you fought just now. He will often make new assaults to recover the honor he has lost. Fight manfully and do not doubt that you have my help."

"You belong to me no more"

After this vision, Francis experienced deep spiritual peace. He now had but one desire, namely, to break off definitely with the world as soon as he could. He made application at once to the Father Provincial of the Capuchins to be admitted. He was accepted, and the date fixed at the friary for his entrance was January 6, 1903.

An interior voice clearly perceived during a thanksgiving after Holy Communion, confirmed the choice he had made and reinforced his fervor.

But on the eve of his departure Francis felt deep pangs over the final separation; for he must now sever himself forever from his family. And how greatly he loved them! How would he manage to cut himself off? The mere thought of it keenly upset him.

But during the night, instead of having the pangs he had feared, he had the comforting surprise of another heavenly vision. Jesus and Mary appeared to him and encouraged him. They assured him of their special affection and they said they were assigning him "a very great mission" known only to God and himself. Our Lord placed His hand upon Francis' head, bestowing on him a special strength to be detached from his family.

The next morning Francis and two other aspirants for the religious life, with Caccavo his schoolmaster, set out from Pietrelcina for Morcone. Francis was then experiencing peace and strength on account of the vision. But how much he suffered when he bade farewell to his mother, sisters, and brother! His mother also deserves our admiration. When bidding him farewell she added something that reveals her noble faith: "Now you belong to me no more, but to St. Francis." She would have liked to say more, but could not, on account of her struggle to hold back the tears.

Later, when Padre Pio would speak of his mother, he would always call her "my holy mother." This fitted her; for Mamma Giuseppa was a woman of uncommon faith, and was humble, wise, generous, and lovable, and enjoyed the favor and honor of having an extraordinary son.

The friary at Morcone was in an isolated place and its atmosphere was favorable for a life of prayer. One of the aspirants, judged to be too young, returned to

Pietrelcina with the schoolmaster. Francis and the other received a warm welcome from the friars. After some refreshment they visited the house, the spacious garden and the beautiful church dedicated to the Madonna delle Grazie, Our Lady of Grace. At last Francis was where he had longed to be. From that moment on he no longer belonged to himself or to his village. He belonged to Christ and to the Church.

Fifteen days later, on January 22, 1903, he received the religious habit or garb and began his year of novitiate. Once clothed in the habit of St. Francis, made in the form of a cross, he perceived that from then on his life would be "crucified with Christ" (Gal. 2:19). And that habit had to reflect poverty and roughness just as a cross does, if Padre Pio would later say, "If people knew how tattered the habit was which I put on in 1903... Yet to me it seemed more beautiful than anything else!"

It was the habit of poverty, the habit of the Poverello, the habit of penance. The habit of the cross, the habit of the Seraphic Militia!

Padre Pio would love the religious habit always, passionately. He wore it always day and night. "The habit of St. Francis" he called it and so wore it, with faith and love. When around 1968 the tunic of St. Francis was brought to San Giovanni Rotondo Padre Pio immediately on seeing it was deeply moved, knelt before the relic and venerated it, kissing it in ecstasy and tears.

Starting on that day Francis Forgione began a new life, using a new name, which was Fra Pio da Pietrelcina. He was almost sixteen years old.

"Either penance or hell"

Upon the door of the Capuchin novitiate at Morcone at that time powerful words were written calculated to jolt a man who would enter: "Either penance or hell."

These words told the essential feature of a novitiate—to pass through a sieve of sacrifice that tests whether one is chosen by God. An observant religious life is a life for steadfast, generous souls. It is not for the cowardly and the half-hearted. The religious vocation is a wonderful blessing, but it demands great courage.

The virile, stern feature of Capuchin novitiate life in Morcone flourished then in an extraordinary way, at times reaching some excess, according to statements of some older friars.

But it was precisely this rigor that drew good men to apply. The novitiate was always full. Such a bold challenge is attractive to sound, healthy, pure young men.

One's room showed poverty and frugality. There was a hard bed, on which one slept clothed in his habit. The diet was frugal, food being prepared in a plain, rustic style. During winter the friary was as cold as ice. At midnight one's sleep would be interrupted and fri-

ars would assemble to pray the night office. They always went about sockless and wearing sandals. They took the discipline three times a week; that is, they scourged their bare flesh, reflecting on Our Lord's Passion—but the scourging did not reach the point of injury. The discipline and similar penances were defended by Pius XII on July 9, 1950, who added: "Not all persons, especially in these times, understand this kind of penitential life as they ought. Not everyone holds it in honor as he ought. In fact many today belittle it." (ASS 42: 611).

They fasted during the three Franciscan Lents as well as every Friday of the year. Every day at certain hours they assembled for common prayers. There was much private prayer too, including the times when they laundered their clothing. They kept perpetual silence, except during the short period of recreation in common. They kept their eyes cast down when they went about within the friary as well as outside. All these austere rules and practices made up the life of young novices, who were there to let their spiritual master mold them during this total mortification of the "old man" (Rom. 6:6). There were meditations on the Gospel, on the Passion and Death of Jesus, and on the life of St. Francis. They received instructions on the holy Rule, on the Liturgy, and on good manners and decorum. All this gave solid nourishment and support to the pro-

gram of prayer and penance. All was aimed at leading the novice to fit himself perfectly into a life of love for Jesus Crucified, following the example and footsteps of St. Francis of Assisi.

"A novice beyond reproach"

The Master of Novices, that is, the one having charge of the spiritual formation of the young novices, declared that Fra Pio was "a novice beyond reproach."

If we reflect on the exceptional strictness of novitiate life and then realize that Fra Pio was a novice beyond reproach, we can get an idea of the care about his perfection that good Fra Pio must have exercised continuously during that year.

To be beyond reproach meant that he kept every rule of novitiate life, even the smallest, with a faithfulness that was single-minded and complete.

For example, keeping the eyes always downcast as he went about was something he practiced without failing or faltering. Once when his mother came to see him and brought him little gifts that her motherly heart had contrived, Fra Pio stood before her with eyes cast down and arms folded, with each hand buried in the opposite sleeve.

His mother was grieved and departed with a sad heart. She could not understand why Francis acted that

way. "If I had known he would act that way," she said, "I would not have gone there at all."

When she told everything to his father, Grazio, who had just returned from America, he decided to go at once to see Francis before the boy wrecked his health or perhaps became mentally unbalanced. When Grazio arrived at the Morcone friary, he was pleased to learn that Fra Pio had behaved as he did only in order to observe faithfully the discipline of the novitiate and not because he had poor health or was becoming unbalanced.

We are certain that Fra Pio was uncompromising and totally dedicated in his determination to be an observant religious. He allowed himself no half-way measures. Self-denial, mortification of the senses, patience and perseverance, careful observance even in little things—in all respects he was fully in earnest and was moved by a spirit of deep piety and generous love. His promptness in obeying, for example, was such that when the superior was beginning to give an order, even before he had finished giving it, Fra Pio had already gone to carry it out. No compromises and no half-heartedness. He was giving his all to the limit without holding back. In this way Fra Pio prepared for his religious profession, which he was to make at the end of his year of novitiate.

On Friday, January 22, 1904, before the image of Our Lady of Grace, Fra Pio consecrated himself to God as a victim by making his profession of the three vows

of obedience, poverty, and chastity, as a follower of the Seraphic Father St. Francis.

Toward the priesthood

Now that his novitiate was finished, Fra Pio went back to his studies in preparation for the priesthood. In those days the students were sent wherever the teaching friars were stationed. During his six years of preparation for the priesthood Fra Pio was at S. Elia a Pianisi in Campobasso, then at San Marco la Catola in Foggia, then at Serracapriola in Foggia, and from there he went to Montefusco in the Province of Avellino.

In all these friaries religious life was carried on in practically the same way. Everywhere there was the same austerity, the same poverty, the same solitude, with the daily timetable and customs according to Capuchin tradition; and these he had learned so well during his novitiate that he would never forget them, even in old age. Needless to say, he applied himself to his studies with great diligence. As he was making every effort to be fully faithful, even to the point of scruple, to the austere Capuchin life, and working so zealously at his studies, it is easy to understand why Fra Pio's health began to fail him.

Worried about his health, his superiors agreed to his taking a rest in his home town of Pietrelcina in the hope that the wholesome air would restore him.

In spite of delicate health, Fra Pio went ahead with wonderful perseverance with his class-work, either studying with professors or studying by himself, and thus succeeded in his progress toward the priesthood. Some students might have become discouraged, but not Fra Pio. For him, every bit of progress meant a cross, of greater or lesser weight. This included studies.

One time he had a professor who was over-demanding to the point of absurdity. It was Father Justin of San Giovanni Rotondo, who suffered from undue scruples that were almost an obsession, going so far as to undertake to say his office while holding a rock in his hand when he was drowsy, so that if he dozed off it would fall and wake him up.

Once Father Justin heard Fra Pio's confession and kept him three hours on his knees. When his companions saw him coming out they were astonished and asked what had happened. Fra Pio answered that the confessor had enumerated and explained to him all the sins that could be committed throughout one's life.

Prayer, tears, penance

After the period of temporary profession, Fra Pio made the profession of his solemn and perpetual vows. The ceremony was at S. Elia a Pianisi on January 27, 1907. He was almost twenty years old. His health was

not good; but this did not stand in the way of his vocation; in fact, it made his sacrifice a fuller offering of himself to trials and sufferings of soul and body.

It may seem strange to say so, but the periods he had to spend in his native Pietrelcina for reasons of health, these periods brought on suffering. Having fondly committed and accustomed himself to the routine of Capuchin life, when he was away from any friary he felt like a fish out of water.

This situation began to create delicate problems that caused him to suffer those terrible spiritual trials known as undue scruples, especially about holy Communion. His health became worse. Some thought he suffered from consumption and that his condition was hopeless. Some sought to avoid him for fear of contagion. But in the midst of many trials, the Lord granted him some extraordinary graces. He wrote his spiritual director, Father Benedict, a friar of great intelligence:

"Jesus began to favor his poor creature with heavenly visions not long after the year of novitiate..." We know that Fra Pio's prayer life was fervent and intensified, especially his meditation on the Passion of Christ. This was often accompanied by tears that not only bathed his face, but trickled down on his kneeler and on the floor.

One day his spiritual father asked the reason for this weeping. Fra Pio replied, *"I am weeping for my sins and the sins of all men."* He prayed a great deal.

When living in a friary, his prayers extended beyond the hours of the community prayers. It was a common thing to find him in the choir when he was not in his room. From then on he wanted to recite many Rosaries. One of the resolutions he wrote was to pray fifteen Rosaries a day.

He ventured to compete with another friar, Fra Anastasio, and pledged himself to say more Rosaries. One night he heard someone moving about in the next room. He woke up and thought Fra Anastasio made the noise and was still up reciting Rosaries. So Fra Pio got up, too, to say some more Rosaries, to keep up his competition.

Eventually from his window he called Fra Anastasio. Looking out to Fra Anastasio's window sill he saw there an enormous black dog with eyes glowing like embers. Fra Pio was petrified. The beast took a big leap to a nearby roof and disappeared.

Fra Pio fell on his bed, feeling faint. The next day he learned that the adjoining room had been vacant. Fra Anastasio was occupying another one.

When, for reasons of health, he was staying at Pietrelcina, besides being faithful about his prayers and being diligent in his studies, he endeavored the best he could to observe the Capuchin program of life. He never failed to take the discipline three times a week, even if, in his home town, it could not be always concealed com-

pletely, because certain boys took delight in spying on him. Also, young priests thought he went too far in his asceticism and sympathized with him only because he was ill.

Once, for example, he accepted a strong correction from Don Giuseppe Orlando because Giuseppa, Fra Pio's mother, had complained that her son, instead of using his cot, preferred to sleep on the floor and to use a stone as a pillow. Both in sickness and in health Fra Pio would not take things so easy as to neglect what was needed by way of self-sacrifice and victimhood.

Priest and victim

Fra Pio had good reasons to judge that God specially called him to become a priest and victim.

Consequently he made it his goal to satisfy what seemed God's will, and he put every effort into this two-fold pursuit. But the more he devoted himself to this, the more he felt his health getting worse.

By now he was no longer hoping for a cure, and it did not matter to him if he died, if the Lord so willed. However the lights and advice he had received about God's design for him led him to humbly and ardently wish to celebrate holy Mass at least once, if God so willed. He would be happy to die after that.

He knew that, for serious reasons of health, priestly ordination could be given in advance to one who petitioned it. His superiors were favorably disposed to the idea; for they were very worried and feared his death was approaching.

Fra Pio received the diaconate on July 18, 1909, and submitted a petition at that time for an early ordination to the priesthood. He at once received a favorable response.

He passed his examinations for ordination at the diocesan curia in Benevento and was accepted for the priesthood. The long-awaited day was approaching, and he prepared himself for that great event with intense prayer. Both fear and joy filled his young heart.

He is raised to the priesthood

At last, on August 10, 1910, Fra Pio was ordained a priest at the cathedral in Benevento by the bishop, Msgr. Paolo Schinosi. Among those present were his mother, whose heart was full, his sisters and brother, and the archpriest of Pietrelcina, Don Salvatore Pannullo. His father, unfortunately, was not there; for he had gone to America the second time to remedy the economic needs of his family.

Padre Pio was not apt to ever forget what he felt during his priestly ordination and throughout that ex-

traordinary day. Nor could it be otherwise if we reflect on the ardent ideals that had moved him and sustained him through a thousand difficulties, to bring him to this event of sublime grace. Now his heart could not fail to appreciate the blessing of the priesthood indelibly imprinted in his soul.

Four days later, on the vigil of the Assumption, he sang his first high Mass in the church at Pietrelcina at the altar of the Madonna. Father Agostino, his theology professor, delivered the sermon. Addressing the new priest he said, "Your health is not good; so you cannot become a preacher. My hopes for you are that you will be a great and conscientious confessor." The utterance was prophetic and was fulfilled in an awe-inspiring way.

On that day Padre Pio wrote a short prayer, which could be considered a program for priestly holiness:

"O Jesus, Object of my longings and my life, I ask Thee as I lift Thee up today in the Sacrament of love, to enable me to be a holy priest and a perfect victim for Thy sake."

"If you want to assist at Mass with devotion and with fruit, think of the sorrowful Mother at the feet of Calvary".

THE WONDERWORKER PRIEST

His stay in his home town bears fruit

After his ordination Padre Pio spent about six years in Pietrelcina for reasons of his health, which was always poor. Each attempt to restore him to religious life in a friary was unsuccessful. His priestly life at Pietrelcina followed a well-ordered plan. It included much prayer, with religious functions, theological studies, the teaching of catechism to children, and meetings he held with individuals and with families.

Something truly providential was his encounter with his former schoolmaster, the unfortunate ex-priest Domenico Tizzani. When it became known that Tizzani was about to die, no one had the courage to approach him. His daughter, almost in despair, managed by chance to tell Padre Pio about it, who was passing by Tizzani's residence. Padre Pio at once asked to be allowed to visit the sick man. He entered, and he brought him the grace of God and eternal salvation for his soul. The dying man made his confession with earnest tears of repentance, and Padre Pio also wept with joy.

Padre Pio's whole day was divided between time spent in church, at home, in the tower room, and out

on the countryside of Piana Romana seated beneath an elm, recollected as he prayed his breviary and many other prayers.

He has diabolical and supernatural encounters

Beneath that Elm tree (enclosed today within a chapel) Padre Pio suffered many furious assaults from the devil, who used to appear to him in various guises. "Nobody knows what used to happen there at night," he later said, indicating by swings of his hand the blows he received.

A phenomenon even more mysterious had its origin in 1910 near the elm. Padre Pio describes it in a letter to his spiritual director: "In the middle of my hands a red spot appeared, having almost the size and form of a centesimo coin, accompanied by a sharp pain. This pain was more perceptible in the middle of the left hand, and it continues still. Also I feel a bit of pain on the bottoms of my feet."

This suffering in his hands and feet is the first record of Padre Pio's stigmata, which were invisible until 1918. Eventually they often caused him to suffer "very sharp pain." One time when he was entering his home his hands trembled as though they were on fire. His mother noticed it, and asked, "What is this? Do you play the guitar?" She did not know the mystery about his hands. Padre Pio made no reply.

One of the painful phenomena rather frequent in Padre Pio's life were assaults made on him by devils, whom he preferred to call "ugly monsters" and "impure fiends." There were not only interior assaults made, but also exterior ones, accompanied by noises, tremors, howls, and flying objects. Padre Pio described one of these assaults as follows to his spiritual director:

"It was late at night and they began their assault with devilish noise. Although I saw nothing at first, I understood who was producing the strange sound. Instead of getting terrified, I prepared for the battle by facing them with a sneering smile. Then they came before me under the most detestable appearances. To get me to abuse God's grace, they began to treat me with kid gloves. But thank heaven I told them off good, and dealt with them according to what they were worth. And when they saw their efforts go up in smoke they hurled themselves on me, threw me on the floor, and gave me terrific blows, throwing into the air pillows, books, and chairs, at the same time letting out desperate cries and uttering extremely filthy words."

One who goes to Pietrelcina to visit the places frequented by Padre Pio can see the room where the furious assault happened. Sometimes the assaults would be renewed several nights in succession. It would also happen that the blows would be so hard and numerous that they made him bleed at the mouth and cause serious fears for his life. "They beat me so brutally," Padre Pio said later, "that I think it was a very great

grace that I was able to stand it without dying." His spiritual director summed up as follows the different forms of diabolical harassment that Padre Pio suffered during his life:

> *"The devil would appear in the form of an ugly black cat, or as a naked young woman performing an impure dance, or as a prison-guard who would whip him, or even in the guise of Christ Crucified,... or of his spiritual father,... of his Father Provincial, etc. At other times it was in the guise of his Guardian Angel, of St. Francis, of the Madonna.[4]"*

Padre Pio knew it was his task to live continually in a state of warfare. The vision he had as a boy of fighting the black giant, with the Lord at his side helping him so that he defeated the giant—this vision enlightened Padre Pio about his whole future of struggles against Satan. "He will always be making new assaults," his Guide had told him, adding, "Fight manfully and do not doubt that you have my help."

To us Padre Pio recommends constant vigilance, "because", as he said,

> *"the devil is always awake, never asleep!"*

Wounds, ecstasies, talks with angels

In addition to suffering from the diabolical, Padre Pio received graces and some of the remarkable gifts

which God grants to certain of His Saints. These are mystical phenomena, interior and exterior, spiritual and bodily, which make the creature more and more like Jesus.

On August 12, 1912, there was the mystical experience of a "wound of love." Padre Pio wrote as follows to his spiritual father:

"I was in church making a thanksgiving after Mass when all of a sudden I felt my heart wounded by a dart of hot, blazing fire, so that I thought I was going to die..."

Often after assaults from Satan he was comforted, sometimes "two or three times a day," by ecstasies and apparitions of Jesus, the Blessed Virgin, his Guardian Angel, St. Francis of Assisi, and other Saints. Some conversations during the ecstasies were recorded and they reveal Padre Pio's great charity in the interest of the salvation of souls, and his burning love for "sweet Jesus," his tender fondness for the Madonna, whom men "would call a goddess" if their faith did not teach otherwise.

Padre Pio showed great devotion for his Guardian Angel. Something interesting occurred in this regard which he told in a letter to his spiritual father:

"...Saturday it seemed that the devils wanted to finish me off with their blows and I did not know what Saint to turn to. Then I called on my guardian Angel, who, after making me wait a while, was right there at last to help me, and with his angelic voice he sang hymns to the Divine

Majesty. I complained to him for making me wait so long, for I had not neglected to call him for help. To punish him, so to speak, for being late, I tended to avoid looking him in the face and to move away from him. But he, poor thing, came up to me almost in tears, so that I lifted up my eyes, looked him in the face, and saw that he was all distressed[5].

Then he told me, 'I am always near you, dear friend (mio diletto). I always walk near you... This love I have for you will not end, even when you die.'

Padre Pio lived in intimate contact with his Guardian Angel, who enabled him to translate letters written in Greek and French. He used to keep Padre Pio up at night to chant God's praises with him. He used to ease the pain Padre Pio suffered from the beatings he took from demons. This Angel thus became his help-mate, and would carry messages from him to souls far away, bringing them comfort and a blessing.

One time Padre Pio wrote this about his Angel:

"Oh, the poor dear! He is too good. Does this not make me see my grave obligation of gratitude?"

Padre Pio counselled many of his spiritual children to engage their guardian angel in some way, to entrust tasks to him, to have him go to Jesus and to the Madonna, to this or that person. In his striking way of speaking, he encouraged them to get their guardian angel to "fly" so as not to let "his wings rust."

Departure from Pietrelcina

After staying in Pietrelcina nearly seven years, on February 17, 1916, Padre Pio departed for Foggia, having been summoned by his superior to render a spiritual service.

A chosen soul, Raffaelina Cerase, was near death and had requested his assistance. She had "offered herself as a victim" to God "that Padre Pio might return permanently to the friary and by hearing confessions bring great benefit to souls." This is a statement which his spiritual director left us in writing.

We can rightly believe that it was precisely because of this woman's generous offering of herself that from then on Padre Pio could stay permanently at the friary and could undertake that ministry of mercy and pardon that was to reach an almost countless number of souls. Distance, however, would never be able to banish Pietrelcina from his heart, "because," he said, "Jesus was there and everything has happened there."

A few years before his death Padre Pio spoke again to some persons from Pietrelcina:

"I have detailed recollections of Pietrelcina, rock for rock. Our town ought to be dear to our hearts. Do everything to make it a model town. It is not just by accident that God lets us be born in one place rather than in another. Everything is providential. God's will extends to everything. It is up to us not to stand in the way of God's

designs, who desires his children's glory. He would, in fact, also bring glory to their native soil and its people."

What would Assisi be today if St. Francis had not cooperated with God's design? Every Saint stands as a glory to God and to his native soil.

One day Padre Pio told some people from Pietrelcina:

"I ask one thing of you: let us not let our town disappear."

He used to express this love for his home town by showing joy when fellow townsmen came to see him, and he was interested in all the news about Pietrelcina.

During the second World War when troops occupied Pietrelcina, to those who appeared very worried he said, "Be at peace. Pietrelcina will be preserved as the pupil of my eyes!" And the occupying troops departed from Pietrelcina.

He was very pleased when he learned that a Capuchin friary and seminary had been opened at Pietrelcina. When one of his spiritual sons showed him a brief film on the town, Padre Pio was moved to tears and said, "I thank you, my son." We need to recall here one of his prophetic statements, namely, "During my life I have cherished San Giovanni Rotondo. After my death I will cherish Pietrelcina."

Satan visits his room

At Foggia, Padre Pio "very happily took his place as a religious among his fellow friars, with whom he was always cheerful and witty," according to his superior's account.

At first, he spent his days in prayer and study. His holy Mass was very lengthy and devout, and he paid a daily visit to the shrine of the Madonna of the Seven Veils, where St. Alphonsus Liguori once had a famous ecstasy while delivering a sermon.

Not much time passed before a "throng of souls" needing help and guidance began to gather around Padre Pio. This is what he wrote to his spiritual Father: "You need to know that I am not left free for one minute. A throng of souls thirsting for Jesus deeply concern me as I run my hands through my hair wondering what next."

Meantime he had painful and strange ailments; that is, lack of appetite, spells of vomiting and perspiring. Most noteworthy were his periods of high fever that baffled all the physicians, who did not know how to treat him. Something even more strange began happening. It was mostly in the evening when Padre Pio was in his room. Loud thuds would be heard that frightened the friars. When they would rush to Padre Pio's room they would find him "drenched in perspiration, and his garments had to be changed from head to foot."

Putting him under obedience to answer, the Father Superior asked the reason for the uncanny noises. Padre Pio replied that the devil was exerting all his powers to tempt him, and the two of them had a fierce battle. He concluded, "By God's grace, I always win. But as soon as Satan is defeated, in his rage he causes a racket."

Certain new arrivals at the friary would not believe the report of such strange goings-on, but laughed at it as a product of some friar's imagination. Once Msgr. Andrea D'Agostino, Bishop of Ariano Irpino, was a guest at the friary. He regarded the friars' story as a fabulous medieval tale. But while he was taking supper with them, a great rumbling noise in the ceiling startled him. He turned pale and trembled. It was not long before he became convinced that the friars' accounts were true.

In the meantime Padre Pio, after being tormented by an assault from the devil, had a wonderful mystical experience—a visit from heaven, an ecstasy. At times he seemed to be someone afflicted almost to the point of despair, who day and night would crave death. At other times he seemed like another St. Francis of Assisi or St. Teresa of Avila, and so surfeited was he with consolation from God that he "got indigestion," as he used to say. And so, as he at turns experienced painful trials and unspeakable joys, he continued always to climb the steep slope of Mount Calvary.

On the Gargano peninsula

On July 28, 1916, Padre Pio came to San Giovanni Rotondo for the first time.

It was an out-of-the-way village on the Gargano peninsula. It consisted of a few poor homes without plumbing, without electricity, with no sewer system. There were no paved roads nor modern means of communication. The place was isolated and unknown to the rest of the world. Village life was frugally austere and unexciting. It was like many villages of those times.

The Capuchin friary was two kilometers outside the town. One reached it by a mule-track that was much-used by shepherds with their flocks. Even more isolated than the town, the friary with its little church, Santa Maria delle Grazie, reflected the poverty and ruggedness of the surrounding terrain, which was rocky and craggy and gave an impression of bleakness. Capuchins had lived there since 1540.

At San Giovanni Rotondo, where Padre Pio was to spend so much of his life, the things that were noteworthy to see included the small church with its lovely Fourteenth Century oil painting of the Madonna delle Grazie, and the restful view of the Gulf of Manfredonia and of the town of Siponto, which borders on the plain known as Delle Puglie. In 1575 St. Camillus de Lellis, who was working in Manfredonia, came up to this fri-

ary. On his return journey, February 2, his wonderful conversion had its beginning.

Padre Pio made his first trip there at the invitation of the Father Guardian of San Giovanni Rotondo, who had come to Foggia to preach, where Padre Pio happened to be stationed. His visit to San Giovanni Rotondo was brief, from July 28th to August 5th, 1916. It pleased the Father Provincial, who hoped for some improvement in Padre Pio's health, and Padre Pio did, in fact, gain some benefit.

On August 13th of the same year, Padre Pio wrote his Father Provincial, proposing that it might be well that he be sent again "to spend a little time at San Giovanni Rotondo," since the place had been beneficial to his health. The Father Provincial then sent him there "under obedience." So Padre Pio was there again on September 4th "for a short time, for some relief and rest, to get a little mountain air." It was to be temporary, for a rest that would serve the health of his body and spirit.

But the Lord fools us when he is designing wonderful things. Padre Pio was to stay at San Giovanni Rotondo for the next fifty-two years, until his death in 1968. The short rest became a heavy toil and sacrifice that unaided human powers could not have borne.

The Army calls

There was an interruption in Padre Pio's stay at San Giovanni Rotondo. It was his call to enter the army during World War I (1915-1918).

On December 18, 1916, he had to appear at Naples. He had been assigned to the Tenth Medical Corps. However, as he was very ill, he was given a leave of absence to regain his health. When he was called back a little later, he was given another period of leave on account of illness. He came back to Naples for the last time on March 5, 1918, and after a few days was given a permanent discharge for reasons of health. His condition had become so serious that one of the medical officers rendered this judgment: "Let us send him home to die in peace."

His discharge papers carried the statement that "his conduct had been good and he had served with loyalty and honor."

Padre Pio, joking, would describe that time as his "hundred days" of military life.

Once, however, he barely missed facing charges of desertion. The summons to military service had not been delivered to him in time because the Postman at San Giovanni Rotondo did not know that Francis Forgione was Padre Pio.

Padre Pio appreciated the duty of a citizen to serve his country. He certainly could have had no wish to

shirk this duty. Indeed he wrote these patriotic words to his spiritual Father:

> *"We ought to do our whole duty according to our ability. The order that comes from authorities we will accept with a peaceful mind and courage. If our country calls us, we ought to obey her. If this call imposes painful trials on us, we accept them with resignation and courage. We might even shed tears at the pain that tortures us, but let them be tears shed with resignation. The trial is hard on everybody, but more than ever it is hard on us. But we lift our hearts to heaven, to God. From Him strength, peace, and comfort will come. At this serious hour we all have to cooperate for the common good and render the Lord's mercy favorable to us by praying humbly and fervently and by amending our lives."*

On the other hand his time spent in the army was very painful to Padre Pio, a "rugged schooling period." It also distressed him because he could not always celebrate his daily Mass. The bad language and blasphemies uttered among soldiers must have torn his heart and affected his health. He had serious fears that he would die there, "departing from this world not in the cloister, but in barracks."

But he had a foreboding, and after repeatedly offering his prayers and trials to God, he said that the end of the tragic war was not far off.

Heart of a watchful Father

At San Giovanni Rotondo Padre Pio served as spiritual director of the boys that made up a small seraphic seminary. Confessions, meditations, and spiritual conversations with these boys kept him occupied day after day. To this task he added much time in prayer and a constant watchful care of their spiritual profit. Desiring their greater good, he ventured to ask his spiritual Father if he, Padre Pio, could offer himself as a victim of the Lord for the perfection of this group, which, he said, "I love tenderly and for which I do not spare myself personal hardship."

Indeed hardship and pains came to him from the devil, who was envious of the profit the boys were gaining. One night a boy was awakened by scornful laughs and the noise of iron pieces being twisted about and dropping on the floor, and of chains knocking against the floor," while Padre Pio was heard to continuously sigh, "O my Madonna!"

The next morning the boy looked at the ironwork that supported the curtain around Padre Pio's bed and found all the pieces twisted. He looked at Padre Pio and saw him "with a swollen, sick-looking eye."

News of this circulated among the boys, who put insistent questions to Padre Pio. He replied, explaining what had happened, but this was only to convince

them of the necessity of prayer in the battle with the tempter. He said,

"You want to know why the devil gave me a terrific beating? It is because I, as your spiritual Father, am willing to defend one of you." Identifying the boy by name, he continued, *"He was suffering a strong temptation against purity, and when he called on the Madonna, he was spiritually also calling on me for help. I rushed at once to assist him, and with the help of Our Lady's Rosary I was successful. The boy that had been tempted slept until morning, while I went through the battle, suffered the blows, but won the fight."*

Another time he accompanied the boys on a walk. But he appeared very serious and sorrowful. The boys gathered around him and insisted that he tell them what was the matter. Padre Pio broke into tears as he said,

"One of you has stabbed me in the heart."

The boys were deeply shaken up, but ventured to ask him for an explanation.

Very sorrowfully, Padre Pio said,

"Just this morning one of you made a sacrilegious Communion! And—to think!—I was the very one to give It to him during the conventual Mass."

Immediately one of the boys fell on his knees in tears and said, "I was the one."

Padre Pio had him get up on his feet, made the others go some distance away, and he heard the boy's con-

fession then and there on the street, in order to restore him to the grace of God.

With a pierced heart

One of the most extraordinary events in the spiritual life of Saints is the phenomenon called "transverberation," which the Spanish mystic, St. John of the Cross, calls, "the seraph's assault." This mystical phenomenon is a supernatural gift of grace which different Saints have received, among whom was St. Teresa of Avila, who has left us a description of the experience and nature of transverberation.

The heart of the person chosen is pierced through by a mysterious arrow or dart in a way that is felt, and one is left with a wound of love which in some way burns, while the soul is raised to the highest contemplation of love and of sorrow.

Padre Pio, too, received this extraordinary grace. With great simplicity he gives a description of it in a letter of August 1918 to his spiritual Father. He writes:

"I was hearing our boys' confessions during the evening of August 5th when, all of a sudden, I was extremely terrified at the sight of a heavenly visitor who appeared before the eyes of my mind. In his hand he held something looking like a long iron rod with a sharp point. Fire seemed to be coming out of the point.

Seeing all this, and watching this person hurl his pointed rod violently into my soul, was something quite beyond my experience. I barely moaned and felt like I was dying. I told the boy to leave the confessional because I felt ill and did not feel I had strength to continue with him.

This martyrdom lasted without interruption until the morning of August 7th. I do not know how to express what I suffered during that time...

From that day to this I have been gravely afflicted. In the deepest part of my soul I feel a wound that is always open, which puts me in agony. Is not this a new punishment inflicted on me by divine justice?"

What does Padre Pio, after all, think this is? He thinks this is just "a new punishment"! In his humility he cannot think differently. And this is the way God's gifts are safeguarded, by giving to God alone "the honor and glory" (I Tim. 1:17).

His spiritual director wanted to give him some peace by assuring him that all that happened was only "the effect of love. It is a trial; it is a call to co-redemption"— that is, a call to share in Christ's work of redemption. "Kiss the hand that pierced you," he added, "and sweetly press to yourself that wound, which is a seal of love."

The marks of Jesus

It is the supernatural phenomenon of the stigmata, chiefly, that has brought Padre Pio world fame. The mysterious fact that he bore in his body the five wounds of the crucified Christ has drawn countless throngs of souls to Padre Pio.

Pope Paul VI magnificently described the reality of the stigmata when he called Padre Pio a representative of Christ on whom are imprinted "the wounds of Christ."

When did Padre Pio get the visible stigmata? How did it come about? He alone can answer these questions because the wonder of the stigmata happened when he was alone on a Friday in the choir for the purpose of making a thanksgiving after a Mass he had just celebrated at the altar of the Immaculata. He had to tell everything "very exactly and out of obedience" to the spiritual Father thirty-two days afterwards in a letter dated October 22, 1918.

He wrote this description of the event:

"It was the morning of the 20th of last month. I was in the choir after celebrating holy Mass, when I was startled out of a peace that was like a sweet dream. All my senses, internal and external, even the faculties of my soul, were experiencing an indescribable quiet. There was total silence around me and within me. Suddenly I felt a great peace and submissiveness to a total detachment from everything. It happened in a flash.

"As it all proceeded, I saw a mysterious visitor before me, like the one I saw on the evening of August 5th; but he differed in that his hands, feet and side were dripping blood. The sight frightened me. I do not know how to express what I felt at that instant. I felt like I was dying, and I would have died if the Lord had not intervened to safeguard my heart, which I felt was bouncing out of my breast.

"Then the vision of the visitor passed away, and I saw that my hands, feet and side were pierced and dripping blood. You will imagine the pain I felt then and that I kept experiencing almost every day continually."

The thing that Padre Pio wanted removed in his stigmatization was not the terrific pain of the wounds, nor the agony of the Passion of his crucified Jesus. It was only the visible marks that he wanted taken away, because they caused him a terrible confusion. He wrote:

"I will strongly raise my voice to Him and will not stop begging Him that in His mercy He take from me not the torture, not the pain—for I see that that is impossible and I feel the will to be surfeited with pain—but I ask the removal of these outward marks that for me mean confusion and indescribable and unbearable humiliation."

The Lord heeded this prayer, but only on his deathbed.

Martyrdom of Medical examinations

Padre Pio's stigmata were deep wounds at the center of his hands and feet and on his left side. His hands and feet were literally pierced all the way through, and fresh blood emerged from both the upper and lower surfaces. He wore half-gloves on his hands and dark stockings on his feet. He put some bandaging on his side, and each night, finding it soaked in blood, replaced it.

Meantime Church authorities were rightly concerned about getting to the bottom of this extraordinary problem so that no doubts would remain about its nature. Therefore they decided that an examination should be made of Padre Pio's five wounds by Professor Bignami of the University of Rome, who was ordinary professor of medical pathology. He was an unbeliever.

Bignami visited Padre Pio for two hours. He admitted the friar's "goodness and sincerity." But he concluded that the wounds might be explained as a morbid pathological occurrence. He judged that the wounds "would disappear after fifteen days" with the care that he would prescribe, strictly carried out under the control of four persons.

However this treatment was perfectly useless. The wounds kept bleeding fresh blood and yielding a fragrance.

At that time there were two other physicians, both believers, who made thorough examinations of Padre

Pio's wounds. They were Doctors Luigi Romanelli and Giorgio Festa. Their conclusions were that Padre Pio's wounds "have an origin which our knowledge is far from explaining. The reason for their existence is something well above human science."

Needless to say, all these medical investigations were a continual torment to Padre Pio. He would have liked to conceal "the secret of the king" from the eyes of all (Tobias 12:7). It was enough to see his face during the examinations; for then he always looked pale and humiliated.

Some years later when he had to have an operation for hernia, Padre Pio ventured to refuse the anaesthetic and made the doctor operate on him when he was fully conscious. This was for fear someone might take the opportunity to get a look at his stigmata. When the surgeon wanted to give him a tiny wine-glass of spirits brewed by Benedictines, Padre Pio would have no more than a taste, and replied in a jesting tone,

"Just a little, as long as Benedictines and Franciscans don't quarrel!"

His suffering during the operation was very great. Padre Pio was perspiring and praying. He carried on heroically, but at the end he fainted. The doctor was then able to examine the stigmata and found them to be completely like fresh wounds.

When he regained consciousness, Padre Pio complained half-joking, half-serious, "Doctor, you betrayed me."

While he was still on the operating table in a room in his friary, someone came to the door and asked him how he was. Padre Pio answered, "I'm keeping this place ready for you."

At that time this person did not understand the meaning of the remark; but he understood it well some days later when unexpectedly he needed surgery, and was in that operating room to undergo the same operation.

Supernatural gifts

If Padre Pio's most extraordinary charismatic experiences were transverberation and the stigmata, we nonetheless must not be silent about his other supernatural gifts that have deeply moved many people. If the transverberation and the stigmata ought to have killed Padre Pio, according to medical judgments, by virtue of his other gifts he was able to show powers which are not given to man naturally to possess—powers which rank him with the most extraordinary Saints and wonder-workers. His gifts of bilocation, of perfume, of prophecy, of reading hearts, of healing, of interpreting languages, of abstaining beyond man's natural powers from both sleep and nourishment—these were a renewal of gifts possessed by St. Francis of Assisi, St.

Anthony of Padua, St. Teresa of Avila, St. Joseph of Copertino, St. Alphonsus Liguori, St. Gemma Galgani, and others.

Did not Jesus foretell that His disciples would "do greater works" than those which He was then performing? (John 14:12) It does not seem exaggerating to apply these words of Our Lord to Padre Pio, for it would be impossible to calculate the sum total of the marvels that occurred in his life.

There are millions of persons who have been in Padre Pio's presence and received spiritual benefit by means of his gift of reading hearts, who have perceived the heavy fragrance that emerges from his person, whose hearts have profited by a miracle worked then and there before them, who have felt themselves powerfully renewed and strengthened in faith and in their will to live the Christian life.

One evidence of all this can be gathered from the fact that one and a quarter miles of mule track leading from the town of San Giovanni Rotondo to the friary has become a broad, paved street, surfaced with asphalt and flanked with hotels, restaurants, apartment dwellings and gardens. What must we say of all the families that have left their homes and home towns in Italy and other countries and transplanted themselves near Padre Pio? What must we say of all the converted souls who owe to Padre Pio the beginning of their new life?

A Pope comments

When Pope Benedict XV learned of Padre Pio's grand array of wonderful gifts and conversion, he said, "Padre Pio is indeed one of those extraordinary men whom God from time to time sends upon earth to convert hearts."

On another occasion the Pope added, "Padre Pio is truly a great soul."

How he succeeded

Padre Pio's gifts have always had this goal, namely to benefit souls and bodies of his fellow men. Through these gifts he strove to attract souls separated from God in order to welcome them back to the true life, to convert them to a true sense of values, and to assist them in their need. He would spread everywhere a ray of light, a warmth of charity, a smile of kindness. He did all this with the greatest naturalness and simplicity, using both playful wit and a stern look. Who can forget Padre Pio's kind humor and his rustic sternness which was also kind? "Mother could not make me sweeter, nor could she make me sterner," he once wisecracked.

By the help of divine grace both his sweetness and his sternness helped souls that approach him. One might say that everything was grace in Padre Pio.

A few phenomena out of many:—

The scent—

One day Dr. Romanelli, as he came close to Padre Pio, noticed a heavy fragrance. He was displeased and almost scandalized. A friar with a reputation for holiness who uses perfume! But he soon realized that the scent was not ordinary perfume, and he could not help but give praise to God for it .

Dr. Giorgio Festa's report is all the more surprising because his condition at the time was such that he "had absolutely no use of the sense of smell." He testified that the fragrance came from Padre Pio's blood rather than from his person. It was a "pleasing fragrance, almost a mixture of violets and roses." The doctor adds, "One should consider that of all the parts of the human organism, the blood is the quickest to rot. In any case the blood never gives off pleasing odors."

Furthermore, the scent was attached to things belonging to Padre Pio and to things he had touched, and it would last a long time. Moreover, people used to perceive the fragrance at a distance coming in whiffs, to signify that Padre Pio was present in some manner at that moment. It often served as a hint —later to be substantiated—of some information or protection, a summons, or a reward.

Bilocation—

Bilocation is a miraculous phenomenon that consists of being in different places at the same time. In one place the person is present in his body; in the other, he is there in his spirit clothed with a representation of his body.

A celebrated instance of Padre Pio's bilocation was when he remained at the friary but at the same time was with the General Cadorna, who was being tempted to commit suicide after his defeat at Caporetto. Padre Pio appeared in his tent and persuaded him to lay aside his pistol. When the general, who did not know Padre Pio at all, visited the friary at San Giovanni Rotondo, he at once recognized Padre Pio as the friar who had entered his tent on the night he was tempted. "*This is the friar who came to see me!*"

And Padre Pio chose to remind him explicitly, "*General, that was a rough night we had!*"

Very noteworthy is a testimony of some English and American aviators who flew low over the Gargano peninsula during the last World War to bomb it. They never succeeded. Why? Because they saw out in the open air before them a friar who stretched out his wounded hands and stopped them from dropping the bombs. "With absolute certainty" they recognized Padre Pio later as the friar that had appeared before their planes in flight.

Reading hearts—

The reading of hearts is a gift that appeared very frequently in Padre Pio. He seemed to read souls like an open book. He often read the hearts of penitents and thus could say to each one the words that were the most suitable and effective. Almost always in the confessional, and sometimes outside the confessional, he gave evidence of knowing in advance what a person had to say and also what facts somebody was trying to hide. There are many testimonies about this. Here are some instances attested by Don Nello Castello, a diocesan priest from Padua:—

"I went to confession to Padre Pio at least a hundred times, and from the first it was something that both jolted and enlightened me. I heard him give me counsels that exactly reflected the whole range of my existence, past and future. At times he would surprise me with suggestions unconnected with the sins confessed. But later events made it clear that his counsels had been prophetic.

"In one confession during 1957 he spoke five times with insistence on the same question, using different words, and reminded me of an ugly fault of impatience. Furthermore, he presented the problem in the causes that had provoked it, and described to me the behavior I ought to follow. This happened without my having said a word about the problem. Thus he knew my trouble better than I did and told it with its various circumstances...

"A man from Padua, in order to get to confession to Padre Pio without the eight-day waiting period required

between one confession and another, lied about the number of days since his last confession. Padre Pio sent him away, forcefully pointing out his lie. I went in search of the man and found him along the wall of the friary much dejected. In tears he repeated a number of times, 'I've told lies to everybody during my life, and I thought I could deceive Padre Pio too.'

"From that day on I found him frequently in church at Padua attending Perpetual Adoration. He confided to me that ever since that correction from Padre Pio, he went to holy Mass and Communion every day...

"My experience in connection with Padre Pio's life and activity assures me that, for the most part, his spiritual children have had experiences of his gift of penetrating within them and knowing their spirit—a gift he often demonstrated.[6]"

Cesare Festa, a lawyer and cousin of the physician George Festa, went to visit Padre Pio, whom his cousin had often described.

As soon as they met, Padre Pio said, "You are a mason."

With a tone of loyalty the lawyer answered,

"Yes Father."

"And what is your task as a mason?"

"It is to carry on our fight against the Church on the political level."

There was a brief silence. Padre Pio fixed his eyes awhile on the lawyer, then took him by the hand and

led him aside. Then he talked to him privately with great gentleness about God's goodness, telling him the parable of the Prodigal Son. In the end the mason was on his knees before Padre Pio confessing his sins and begging God's forgiveness.

Festa has declared that he did not see how Padre Pio knew him so well by any natural means.

Prophecy—

The gift of prophecy, in the ordinary sense, is a special power from God whereby certain privileged souls foretell future events by a divine light. Padre Pio had this gift, and when he used it it was always for the spiritual good of souls. The following are two of the many instances of its use:—

In 1944 Professor Settimio Manelli[7] reported to Padre Pio that Hitler was alarming the world by certain frightening sayings: "Come midnight, and there will be no more midnight."— "At midnight I have lost; and a minute after midnight I have conquered."

Hitler was making clear references to the atomic bomb which he hoped to succeed in using in time to level peoples and nations to the ground and massacre them. Though at the time he seemed to be losing the war, he expected to win suddenly by means of the atomic bomb.

On hearing this report from the professor, Padre Pio's countenance became serious. There were some moments of silence and reflection; then he spoke with assurance: "He will not act in time."

And so it happened. Hitler did not succeed in having the atomic bomb ready for launching in time to win the war by means of a planned devastation never before seen on earth. His enemies were winning and, in Europe, won too soon for him to act.

A second instance happened a few years before Cardinal Montini was elected Pope. Alberto Galletti, who belonged to the nobility in Milan and was a spiritual son of Padre Pio, asked the holy friar's blessing for his Archbishop, who was Cardinal Montini.

"Not a blessing, but something torrential," replied Padre Pio, "and my unworthy prayer!... You tell the Archbishop that he will become Pope. Have you understood me? You must tell him that! For he must prepare himself." As all know, Cardinal Montini became Pope Paul VI.

Other Powers—

The miraculous cure of Anna Gemma di Giorgi of Ribera in Sicily in 1947 received considerable attention in the local press. Gemma was born blind and her eyes have never had pupils. Specialists in Palermo assured her parents that nothing could be done and that the child would never see. One of Gemma's relatives, a

religious Sister, wrote Padre Pio appealing in Gemma's behalf. Soon afterwards in a dream the Capuchin appeared to the Sister asking, "Where is this Gemma you are appealing for so earnestly, whom you are so anxious to see helped?" Then, in the dream, the sister presented Gemma to him. After making the Sign of the Cross over the child's eyes, the priest vanished.

The morning after the dream Sister received a reply from Padre Pio assuring her of his prayers for Gemma. Then Gemma's grandmother decided to take the child to Padre Pio. They set out in June 1947. Gemma was then seven years old. As she was preparing for her first Holy Communion, the grandmother planned to try to arrange that she receive it from Padre Pio.

During the journey Gemma showed evidence of gaining her sight. But it was after Padre Pio heard her confession and gave her her first Holy Communion, tracing the Sign of the Cross on her eyes with his stigmatized hand, that she proved to everyone's satisfaction that she had fully received her sight.

Gemma later became a religious Sister, a member of the Handmaids of Divine Mercy. Her miraculous ability to see well without the pupils is a lasting witness to the favor and support God gives His stigmatized priest.[8]

A GREAT VICTIM

A perfect son of St. Francis—

"I hear a voice within me that persistently tells me, Be holy and have a holy influence." *Padre Pio wrote those words in 1922, summing up the two-fold mission of his life, namely, to develop holiness in himself and to make others holy.*

A few years later, before a group of scientists gathered at a congress, Padre Pio spoke of every man's mission on earth, and said concerning himself:

"What must I tell you? You, too have come into the world as I have, with a mission to accomplish... I, a friar and a priest, have a mission. As a friar, as a Capuchin, it is the perfect and devoted observance of my Rule and vows. As a priest, my mission is one of propitiation, of winning God's favor for the human family."

Every man's vocation is the path traced out for him by God. Padre Pio wanted to sanctify himself as a religious and priest in order to sanctify others. His Franciscan and priestly vocation put him in the following of St. Francis and Christ the High Priest.

For sixty-five years he was a son of the Poverello of Assisi and lived "the perfect and devoted observance"

of the Holy Rule. He died after renewing the profession of his vows a final time. He loved St. Francis with great veneration and devotion.

Thus he strove to imitate St. Francis' devotion to Jesus Crucified, to the Divine Infancy of Jesus, and to Christ in the Eucharist. He also endeavored to imitate St. Francis' efforts to be a "little" ("minor") friar, and that sincere humility that made Francis say, "I am the greatest sinner in the world."

When his spiritual children extended warm congratulations to Padre Pio on his completion of sixty years of religious life, he broke into tears, saying, "Sixty years of unworthiness!"

What shall we say of Padre Pio's love for the poverty of St. Francis? People said that Padre Pio was a saint who was both "beggar and multimillionaire." This is true. Many millions came his way, but went to the service of charity. For himself there was only the poverty of the humble friary and the humble room which hemmed him in for fifty-two successive years.

For him there was no taking time off for trips, no amusements, no ease and comfort. For many years his bedding was a straw mattress over a plank. Each night he would prepare it for use with his cane.

During his last years when they put a sink, a radiator and an air-conditioner in his room, he protested that he absolutely did not want such things. He sorrowfully

complained, "What would our Seraphic Father say?"

Concerning Padre Pio's obedience we can say that his whole life bore out his heroic submission through the many hard trials to which he was subjected. There are two expressions used by Padre Pio that tell the whole story of his obedience: "I am a son of obedience. If my superiors order me to jump out of the window, I will do it without arguing."

And the sweet, powerful scent that came from Padre Pio's person—was it not a song praising his angelic chastity? A writer relates that one time he managed to kiss Padre Pio's shoulder when he was slowly passing through a crowd. The same writer then got inebriating, dense whiffs of the fragrance.

We certainly would not approve of anyone who would try to tear, cut, or carry away a piece of Padre Pio's habit while he passed through a crowd. But how can one fail to see that the attraction for that Franciscan habit, bathed in blood and a mysterious fragrance, offered a powerful temptation, at times almost irresistible? Padre Pio had a special love and veneration for the Franciscan habit that he wore. He even thought himself unworthy to wear it, and once said, "I do not know why this habit of St. Francis that I wear does not fly away from me." He always wore it, day and night. Only during his last years, to be obedient, he took it off in order to rest at night. But he wanted to die clothed

in the habit, and did die in the habit, like St. Francis, who died in his.

We are familiar with Padre Pio's special love for the Madonna. It was a tender, ardent love, like that which the Seraphic Father St. Francis had. We also know about Padre Pio's special devotion to St. Michael the Archangel and his guardian angel. In these respects, too, he was an imitator of St. Francis.

We also find in Padre Pio a warm, devoted zeal in behalf of the Franciscan Third Order. He was Director of a local Third Order group called the Brotherhood of Santa Maria delle Grazie. He remarked in a letter that he considered the Third Order a great means "to enable mankind to return to the light of the faith and to the sound principles of Christian morality."

"A poor friar who prays"

One day a journalist asked Padre Pio who he was. He answered meekly and kindly, "I am a poor friar who prays." Pope Paul VI likewise described Padre Pio as a "man of prayer and suffering."

Certainly prayer has been Padre Pio's principal activity. One will find that he had the extraordinary gift of being able to pray always, even when asleep. It is significant that when his spiritual Father asked Padre Pio to redouble his prayers, Padre Pio replied that this

was not possible because his time was "all spent in prayer."

His prayer was vocal and mental, affective and contemplative. Nothing was lacking in his prayer-life. He used to declare the excellence of prayer by quoting this saying of St. Gabriel of the Sorrowful Mother: "A thousand years of glory in palaces of men cannot be worth the sweetness of one hour spent before the tabernacle."

Moreover, he felt so keenly the need of interceding, of appealing in behalf of others, that it became a matter of necessity to him to continuously intercede for his fellow-men before God, so as to cry like Moses on Mt. Sinai, "Either forgive them this trespass, or if Thou do not, strike me out of the book that thou hast written." (Ex. 32:32).

On the other hand, for the crowds of people needing help who flocked around him, what could he give more than his ceaseless prayer and the suffering he bore to the point of much blood? Therefore he prayed not only in choir and in church, but in his room too, in the hallways, in the paths of the garden, by day, by night, in times of joy and times of dryness, when alone and when with others, with words and with loving glances at sacred images.

A good witness of his intense prayer-life was (without Padre Pio wanting it so) the Bishop of Manfredonia, Msgr. Cesarano. He had asked to be allowed to make

an eight-day retreat at Padre Pio's friary. For eight nights in succession, rising at different hours to make a visit to the Blessed Sacrament, he always found Padre Pio tirelessly absorbed in prayer. With this ceaseless prayer he won showers of graces for his fellowmen.

He preferred to lengthen his hours of prayer rather than his hours in the confessional; for he said, "What mankind lacks today is prayer. Padre Pio made it his concern to apply some remedy to this lack. Hence he devoted much of his life to the work of "Prayer Groups" so that more people would be induced to pray and would receive help to pray well. The prayer Jesus taught us was the Our Father, the most divine and the most human of prayers.

Before his death Padre Pio, as a man well accomplished and heroic in his prayer life, wanted to pray the Our Father as a seal of his life of prayer, and he recited it "perfectly aware of his imminent death, with unusual forcefulness and loudly, as he stressed every word."

The prayer he preferred

The prayer combination that Padre Pio preferred was the Holy Rosary. He loved it and recited it so often that he could be called a "saint of the Rosary."

If one did not see Padre Pio at the altar or in the confessional, it was likely one would see him holding

and praying his Rosary. From the time he was a boy he loved the Rosary. His first visit to a Marian shrine was the visit he paid to the shrine of the Madonna of the Rosary of Pompei.

From the time the Madonna appeared at Fatima as the Madonna of the Rosary and urged the Rosary as a powerful prayer for winning every blessing and banishing every evil, Padre Pio adopted the Rosary as the prayer he said ceaselessly and tirelessly day after day. He said,

"If the Holy Virgin has urged the Rosary wherever she has appeared in her (recent) visions, doesn't it seem that we have a special motive for praying it?"

The more the number of his spiritual children grew and spread out, the more he increased the Rosaries he would recite. It was with the Rosary that he banished sickness and obtained graces. He reached the point of reciting, in the course of a day, an inconceivable number of Rosaries. He spoke of the fact a number of times to different people.

These facts bear out principally two things: first, that Padre Pio prayed uninterruptedly, having that mystical gift that some great Saints have had of praying even while asleep or doing other things; second, it seems evident that this uninterrupted prayer was something all Marian, as it all consisted of Rosaries.

Here is something he said that eloquently preaches the excellency of the Rosary:

"I wish days had forty-eight hours so that we could double our Rosaries."

Needless to say, the whole array of gifts and miracles that Padre Pio used for souls, came about through the Rosary. His power to draw sinners and stray souls who came from everywhere, was the fruit of his Rosaries. All his projects and enlightened counsels and his victories over sin were linked with the power of the Rosary.

Ceaselessly praying the Rosary, he also upheld the truth that Mary is Mediatrix of all graces, of which St. Bernard said, "The Lord gives nothing but what passes through the hands of the Queen of Heaven."

Needless to say Padre Pio used to urge people with all his zeal to pray the Rosary. He gave away countless Rosaries. Someone asked him one day what the inheritance would be that he would leave his spiritual children. He answered at once, "The Rosary." Someone else asked him what prayer to choose for use throughout one's life. He promptly replied,

"The Rosary."

Shortly before his death, some of his spiritual children asked him for some words of wisdom. He answered, "Love the Madonna and make her loved by others. Always pray the Rosary."

Day and night Padre Pio used to entrust to the Madonna his spiritual children and his Home for the Re-

lief of Suffering, offering up endless Hail Marys for them
on his Rosary beads.

Victim in the Confessional

To realize, after coming to San Giovanni Rotondo,
that one must wait a month or more to go to confession to Padre Pio—this has been a shock that many
people were not expecting.

But there was nothing one could do about it. One
had to face the presence of the crowds. The time passed
for everybody. Padre Pio was but one person. Though
he followed a fast procedure reduced to essentials, he
was absolutely unable to promptly hear everybody's
confession who came for that purpose.

On the average, a confession made to Padre Pio lasted
only three minutes. He heard about twenty persons an
hour. During a morning and an afternoon he would hear
about sixty women and about sixty men. Thus he heard
over a hundred confessions a day. But this figure certainly does not reveal all. There were long periods in his
life when he heard confessions for ten and even fifteen
hours a day. There have been days when Padre Pio spent
up to nineteen hours hearing confessions.

According to an estimate, Padre Pio heard a total
of about five million confessions. Only God knows the
exact figure. But one thing is certain: Padre Pio was a

martyr of the confessional. Perhaps some day he will be called the Saint of the confessional and rank among the most wonderful confessors the Church has had, alongside the holy Cure of Ars and St. Leopold Mandic.

Calling him an "apostle" and "martyr" of the confessional has been well justified. But it is hard to find a word to fully reflect the extent of the martyrdom that Padre Pio endured every day between the three wooden walls that enclosed him and hid him from the world's eyes.

He felt the full weight of this supernatural role. He once said to a priest, "If you but knew what a fearful thing it is to sit in the tribunal of the confessional! We are administering the Blood of Christ. We must be careful that we do not fling It about by being easy-going or unserious."

A beautiful sight to behold was Padre Pio coming down to hear confessions, and first pausing before an image of the Madonna to pray fervently. He was entrusting his ministry of mercy and pardon to the one who is "full of grace."

Padre Pio was painstakingly faithful to the ministry of confession until the day of his death. On the morning of September 22, 1968, when he was carried into the old sacristy, he heard his seven last confessions—that of seven men. During the night that followed he passed into eternity.

He was concerned about the frequency of confession.

He counted frequent confession important for himself and for others. He made his own confession at least every week, and often several times a week, without counting those periods when he went to confession every day to whatever priest was at hand.

As for others, he wanted weekly confession to serve as a golden rule of the Christian life. Even during the years when great throngs were coming to him, he never wanted his spiritual children to stay away from confession more than ten days.

Once a spiritual daughter had carelessly let a month pass without coming to confession. When she came to Padre Pio and told him that she had not gone to confession for a month, she received a severe rebuke from him.

"Oh, how neglectful! That you would not yet understand the value of confession and what you lost by neglecting this sacrament!"

For Padre Pio was convinced that confession is a powerful means not only for removing sins, but also for increasing divine grace. He taught that an atom of grace is worth more than the whole created universe.

"He takes away the sins of the world."

"What does Padre Pio do?" Pope Pius XII once asked the archbishop of Manfredonia.

"Your Holiness, he takes away the sins of the world," the archbishop replied promptly.

A wonderful answer! He could not have summed up better Padre Pio's apostolic work and mission. He became a martyr-victim of prayer, of sacrifice and of labor in order to deliver "his fellow men from Satan's clutches." And how much Padre Pio loved souls! For their sake he did not count the sacrifice nor the prayers nor the toil. He knew very well that souls cost blood. He said so himself: "Souls do not come as a gift. They are bought. You do not know what they cost Jesus. Today it is always with the same coin that they must be paid for."

Often he would say to his converts, "It was with love and pain that I begot you. How much you made me suffer! I bought you at the price of my blood." This pain was often evident on his face while he recited the sacramental formula of absolution. His lips writhed and he turned pale as he painfully stammered out every word. It seemed that during those moments he was yielding his blood to wash away the sins of the repentant soul!

How explain the fact that Padre Pio denied absolution to so many persons? And why did he often treat

penitents with gruffness? Sometimes he would rebuke penitents with very severe words that he alone knew how to say. For example: "How irresponsible! Why did you sell your soul to the devil? ... How irresponsible! You are on the way to hell! ... O you irresponsible woman! Go away and get dressed! ...O you careless man, go first and get repentance, and then come here...!"

Even these words, however, reveal Padre Pio's love for the welfare of souls. When someone asked him the reason for such strong language, he replied,

> *"I do not give sweets to someone who needs a laxative."*

A soul in need of being shaken up, should not be caressed. And Padre Pio, powerfully endowed with gift of reading hearts, perceived at once what was needed and did not balk about using a means that was both violent and saving, that of refusing absolution or giving a rebuke that sunk like a fiery blade into the center of the soul.

But he suffered, and he suffered a great deal when he was obliged to deny absolution or deal harshly with someone. He once said so in confidence to a priest:

> *"If you knew how I suffer when I have to refuse absolution! ... But it is better to be blamed on earth by a man than in the next life by God."*

Once after he had dealt harshly with a penitent, he confided to a friar,

"If you just knew how my own heart is afflicted before I cause this grief to a fellow man! But if I did not do this, many would not be converted to God."

He rightly demanded that every confession be a true conversion. He could not tolerate superficiality or unseriousness in the use of the sacrament of forgiveness. His treatment hit hard those who made untrue excuses, who showed themselves insincere, who sheltered themselves in compromises, who lacked determination. He required frankness and honesty in the account of one's sins, a sincere sorrow coming from the heart, and a firmness in a penitent's resolutions for the future. Above all he wanted penitents to sincerely acknowledge their sins and their malice.

A penitent tried to excuse his sins by saying, "The temptation was stronger than I was. I did not have the power... I could not resist."

Padre Pio replied, "Here God must be the one to absolve. If you do not realize your guilt and would absolve and acquit yourself, then leave, and do not try my patience."

No one realizes God's goodness and holiness as the Saints do. Therefore no one appreciates as they do the ugliness and evil in every sin. Hence they react strongly and fight all kinds of battles, just to save God from being offended.

If we reflect that Padre Pio had before him and within him, Jesus wounded and crucified by our sins, we are not so astonished at his tears and his indignation toward persons who "crucify Jesus anew in their hearts" (Hebrew 6:6).

Once when he was hearing a confession he began to weep. When asked why, he answered, "I weep at men's ingratitude toward their supreme Benefactor. What more should we have expected Jesus, poor Jesus, to do that He has not done?"

Almost all of Padre Pio's penitents bear witness that in his confessional they used to experience the awesome impression of standing before the judgment seat of God. A young man, after receiving his doctorate, confided to me, "It is less frightening to take a difficult examination at the University, than to go to confession to Padre Pio."

This is the truth. Padre Pio would use the smile or the whip, the caress or the slap with a firm and saving hand. When it was necessary he even gave you a sort of boot; but it was to make you escape a serious danger.

He often wrote things to his spiritual Father that throw light on his whole behavior, when it appears otherwise unexplainable. For example, he once wrote, "How is it possible to behold a God who grieves at sin and not grieve likewise? What do I do when I see God on the point of discharging His thunderbolts, and per-

ceive that there is no other way to ward them off except to raise one hand to hold back God's arm, and to raise our other hand to urgently appeal to our brother to separate himself from evil and leave the way of sin promptly, for the Judge's Hand is about to be lowered upon him?"

There was no blind impulsiveness nor thoughtlessness in Padre Pio's conduct with his penitents. He always worked with the Spirit of God "to root up and destroy" evil and "to plant" good (Jer. 1:10).

It is enough to add that the vast majority of those whom Padre Pio sent away unabsolved, came back sooner or later to him. They could not remain without the absolution of the physician who stood for justice and salvation.

"A world-wide following"

When his spiritual director had need to describe in a few words Padre Pio's day, he wrote that he found him "always occupied either with Jesus or with souls."

In one letter Padre Pio had said he felt "consumed with love for God and love for neighbor." And his life was really lived in the total charity required by the two greatest commandments on which "depend the whole Law and the Prophets" (Mt. 22:40). His day was one of ceaseless prayer for his "brethren in exile"—an expres-

sion he was fond of. Besides long hours spent in the confessional in order to purify and sanctify souls, Padre Pio must have run into many others whom he dealt with kindly; for he used to be literally besieged by people wherever it was possible to approach him. In the sacristy, in the choir, along the stairways, in the hallways, on the veranda, in his room, in the garden— he used to run into little groups or waiting lines of men who wanted a word with him, a reply, a counsel, a friendly smile.

Once someone managed to climb over the wall enclosing the friary garden in order to catch Padre Pio while he was walking under the cypresses.

It was a touching sight to see these men, half hidden at the door entrances of the friary, at the bends of corridors, waiting, often in great anxiety, for Padre Pio to pass their way. Every day after Mass, Padre Pio passed among the men gathered in St. Francis' Hall, called the "sala S. Francesco." He used to chat briefly with some of them, and with a penetrating, fatherly look, he greeted them all.

When one saw him walking along the corridor with pained steps, pausing to speak with one and then with another, saying a word of comfort or of hope, giving his blessing or a word of exhortation, one saw a true imitator of Christ, Who "went about doing good" (Acts 10:38).

We should remember that the men who flocked to Padre Pio often included high-ranking prelates, scholars, celebrated artists and scientists, noted writers, and responsible leaders of society. All were turning to the "man of God" (II Tim. 3:17), who had the gift of knowing people "in and out as you know yourself in the mirror." And Padre Pio used to find the right word and gesture suited for each one—to this one, a word of encouragement; to that one a rebuke; a smile for another; a stern glance for another; an embrace for another; to another he would say, "Leave me, you evil man!" But Padre Pio's association with his fellow man did not end here. A multitude of people would have liked to go to San Giovanni Rotondo in order to approach Padre Pio personally. But oftentimes distance presented too great a difficulty. Persons in the Americas, in Japan, in Poland, in Sweden—how could many of these ever get to San Giovanni Rotondo? There was just one way for them to reach Padre Pio, and that was by letter or telegram. And so year by year the stream of letters that reached San Giovanni Rotondo increased, soon becoming a river, then a flood. On the average about a thousand letters and a hundred telegrams were coming in each day.

The Holy Father Paul VI sharply commented, "Behold, what a fame he achieved! What a world-wide following had gathered about him!"

God is wonderful in His holy ones (Ps. 67:36).

Crucified on the altar

It is something unique in the world and in history for a priest bearing the stigmata to celebrate holy Mass before crowds of people. According to estimates, about twenty million persons have seen Padre Pio celebrate Mass. St. Joseph of Cupertino, who celebrated Mass during ecstasies and levitations, was sheltered and hidden almost all his life. Padre Pio, however, was observed on the altar by countless crowds.

Jesus Crucified and Padre Pio stigmatized made an impressing combination during his holy Mass. The renewal of the Sacrifice of Calvary took place without disunity. The same Jesus was sacrificed upon the Cross and in Padre Pio. This was especially evidenced at the moment of Consecration when Padre Pio stammered out painfully the words of consecration, "Hoc est enim Corpus Meum... Hic est enim Calix Sanguinis Mei."

These words sounded like blows of a hammer upon the nails that pierced the hands and feet of Jesus and Padre Pio.

A remark of Padre Pio discloses his active share in Jesus' crucifixion, which he re-lived at the altar during Mass. When a spiritual daughter asked him how he could manage to stand up throughout the Mass when the wounds on his feet were paining him, Padre Pio replied, "My daughter, during Mass I am not standing

on my feet. I am hanging." Being with Jesus suspended on the Cross— this was Padre Pio's Mass.

Another of his enlightening reflections is this:

"Gethsemani, Calvary, altar! Three places of which the last is the sum of the first two. They are distinct places, but in one only is where you will find yourselves.

He desired on the part of all attentive and devout participation at Mass.

"Silence and on your knees". How many times Padre Pio recommended these two things to those near his altar.

And unforgettable is the scene of those crowds who attended the long Mass of Padre Pio in prayerful silence and devout attention.

His penetrating glances, the unique gestures of his hands, the almost imperceptible movements of his body, his serious and earnest tone, his slow, painful genuflections, the forceful blows he gave his breast at the "mea culpa" and at the "Domine non sum dignus," the mystifying expressions in his face, and his many, many tears—how can one forget these things that were all a part of Padre Pio's Mass?

The writer remember the times that, while serving the Mass, he witnessed Padre Pio's ecstasies, during which his body was as motionless as a statue and his face was transfigured. With another movement or jerk,

likewise almost unnoticeable, he used to come out of it and carry on with the holy Mass. His Mass was something that lived Christ's sorrows and Christ's love, wrapped in mystery; yet it reached the heart, so that Padre Pio gave you a glimpse into the depths of the mystery of his bleeding, of his tears, of his prayer—all ordained to remind you of the suffering Jesus.

He used to prepare for Mass long before daybreak. An entry in the Chronicles of the friary tells us that Padre Pio "rises at about one A.M., makes his preparation for Mass, and at 3:50 he goes down the sacristy... When the time arrives to celebrate Mass he cannot delay..."

He revealed his sentiments on the value of the Mass to a spiritual son and convert of his: "If men only appreciated the value of a holy Mass they would need traffic officers at church doors every day to keep the crowds in order."

Crucified for souls

One day a sturdy, strong gentleman who was a spiritual son of Padre Pio met him in a corridor of the friary and saw that he was exhausted from his terrible suffering. Deeply touched, he went up to him and, moved by a generous impulse, he said, "Padre Pio, give me your sufferings. I am hardy and strong. I will bear them at least for a time."

"You would die like one struck with lightning!" Padre Pio answered at once.

How much did Padre Pio suffer? Who can say? One can only say that his sufferings had to have a limit just as the number of souls entrusted to him had a limit.

Padre Pio did not spare himself in his efforts to save any soul. Once he gave this answer to someone who asked how much he suffered:

"As much as one can suffer who bears all humanity on his shoulders. Pray for one who carries the weight of all, who carries the Cross for everybody!"

But it had been his own doing to offer himself as a victim to pay the debt of sinners. During the year of his priestly ordination he had asked his spiritual Father if he might offer himself as a victim for poor sinners. He asked that "the punishments prepared for sinners might be showered on himself.

And his spiritual Father had replied, "Suffer, sigh, and pray for the sins of the world."

If "mystical substitution" really exists in the spiritual life where an offer is accepted to receive punishment for another's sin, we can thus explain those mysterious ailments and those sudden pains that struck Padre Pio with no evident reason and without any plausible explanation. They were all pains of mystical substitution. He had offered to suffer in place of another.

There were often instances of mystical substitution in the life of St. Veronica Giuliani. The Saint offered to suffer the great pains that souls were suffering in Purgatory in order to enable them to enter paradise at once. Such charity is immense. One who is guiltless pays the penalty for the guilty. Here we find unsullied heroism in love for neighbor. "Greater love than this no man hath, that a man lay down his life for his friends" (John 15:13).

How many times did Padre Pio offer himself in mystical substitution to take away other people's sufferings? God alone can give the answer. We know that "they flocked to him from all sides" and that he never spared himself, allowed himself no respite, and took no vacation of any kind. People saw him active in this role for fifty-two years, an untiring soldier doing battle against Satan's kingdom, a magnificent champion of God's love, totally sacrificing himself day by day "for the sins of the people" (cf. Heb. 7:27).

He showed his conviction to the letter of God's word that "without shedding of blood there is no remission" (Heb. 9:22). As he wrote his spiritual Father, he offered himself totally, without holding back in any way, all so that he might relieve the great needs of his fellow men who had sinned and who suffered.

"I have labored; I want to labor. I have prayed and I want to pray. I have kept watch; I want to keep watch. I have wept and I want always to weep for my brothers

in exile... I am carried away to a point of giddiness with these pains, even though I cannot help wincing."

Again he writes: "If I listened only to the voice of my heart, I would ask Jesus to give me all the sorrows of men."

Crucified by men

Padre Pio's life, as we have seen, has been one painful passion, a succession of trials and sufferings in his body and in spirit. The most painful chapter of this passion is what he had to suffer from men, and mostly from some of his brothers in the priesthood and in the religious life.

The lament of the Prophets was verified in him: "If my enemies had reviled me, I would verily have borne with it... but it was thou... my friend and my familiar" (Ps. 54:13-14). Such things are called for if one is to resemble the crucified Jesus. Jesus was a "sign of contradiction" and forewarned his followers, "If they have persecuted Me, they will also persecute you" (John 15:20). There were two long periods of persecution when men crucified Padre Pio. The first was from 1923 to 1933. The second was from 1959 until his death.

During the first persecution attacks were chiefly made on his person and his ministry. During the second, the attack was on Padre Pio and his great work,

that is, the Prayer Groups and the Home for the Relief of Suffering[9]. During both persecutions there were serious calumnies and accusations against his doctrinal soundness, against his morals, his mental competence, and against his practical prudence. Painful measures were taken. Several attempts were made to transfer Padre Pio from San Giovanni Rotondo to another place. But it always proved impractical. It would have raised a tumult among local people.

From 1923 to 1933 his spiritual director was taken from him, he was forbidden to write letters, and he was required to celebrate his holy Mass in the morning before dawn. During the last two years of this period, Padre Pio was kept secluded in his friary, suspended from hearing confessions and forbidden to have any contact with the faithful. He could celebrate holy Mass only in the little private chapel of the friary with no one present but the server. Things continued this way until July 16, 1933, when he was at last allowed to celebrate Mass again in the church and to resume hearing confessions. But in the meantime Padre Pio had been everywhere eyed with suspicion as a questionable or dangerous person.

From 1959 on, he was subject to an even great persecution. We remember quite well how newspapers and periodicals during those years carried articles on Padre Pio with derogatory headlines and shameful misrepresentations. In order to stop the stream of dona-

tions that supported the Home for the Relief of Suffering founded by him, his persecutors put together a dossier of absurd and ruinous charges, and took the sacrilegious step of putting microphones in his confessional in an attempt to find something blameworthy. Certain offices of the Roman Curia conducted investigations and inquiries. The administration of the Home for the Relief of Suffering was taken out of Padre Pio's hands, and his Prayer Groups were left to languish. The faithful were advised not to assist at Padre Pio's Mass. An iron railing and barrier was set up around his confessional calculated to check the flow of penitents.

One may get a concise idea of what Padre Pio was undergoing from this statement of Cardinal Lercaro made at the time: "They want to put a gravestone over San Giovanni Rotondo. But they have not been successful, because the finger of God is there." This was true, because the holiness and the work of Padre Pio were truly built on rock. Therefore they could not collapse under the storm. His spiritual children, both clergy and laity, became an impressive force of loyalty and of defense for Padre Pio throughout the world. The world-wide following not only did not grow less, but increased uninterruptedly around Padre Pio, and was able to glory all the more in this victim whose life heroically fulfilled Christ's words, "Blessed are they that suffer persecution for justice' sake, for theirs is the kingdom of heaven" (Mt. 5:10).

MESSAGE, WORKS, ETERNITY

He presented God to men

The spread of atheism among the masses is the gravest and most frightening development of our age, during which many men openly deny God's existence, while most people live practically as though there were no God. But God is often making His presence felt, and He discloses His Hand through certain holy souls whom He has chosen as His witnesses in the world. One of the chosen souls that have shown the Creator's power and goodness in a very awesome way is certainly Padre Pio. In this man God has revealed Himself by means of extraordinary phenomena.

To keep living when one's temperature is 118 Fahrenheit is only the work of God. To suffer from five wounds for fifty years that trickle blood every day is only God's doing. To eat so little and take so little sleep is impossible if a man would keep alive. But these things were not impossible for Padre Pio, supported by divine power. What can be said, then, about the other prodigies, like bilocation, prophesying, reading the hearts and minds of others, the unaccountable fragrance and other astonishing facts? They are all gifts

"coming down from above" (James 1:17) that reveal God's presence and power.

Likewise the power to perform cures, to deliver people from many evils, and to work so many miracles for the profit of his suffering fellow men— all this indicates the Hand of the Almighty. But the most impressive and striking thing that shows God's presence and power in Padre Pio has been the conversion of so many sinners and fallen-away souls.

When we see success in overcoming a free creature's stubborn adherence to evil, then we should acclaim the most impressive miracle that can happen. And these miracles of conversion have been very numerous at San Giovanni Rotondo. Humble folk as well as persons of high rank have found God in His faithful servant. Protestants, atheists, masons, communists, anarchists, and agnostics have received at San Giovanni Rotondo the clear, bright light of grace that brought them back to God[10]. And we should not fail to mention that moving around Padre Pio there was a whole world of high prelates, noted scientists and physicians, and talented writers who wrote pages telling of the friar of Gargano. All this is certainly not a normal thing in the life of a poor friar.

Likewise the transformation of San Giovanni Rotondo, now paved with streets, beautified with new homes, villas, and hotels, and famed for its magnificent medical center and many other projects, is an evi-

dence that men have recognized God's full and particular presence in that place where there once lived a man favored and beloved by God.

He asked loyalty to God

Padre Pio has not only shown us God, but what is more he has taught us how we ought to love and serve God. God must be loved whole-heartedly and faithfully, without compromise, without setting limits, without reservations. We must offer Him this for our whole life, in big things and in little things. What Jesus has asked is a love that totally rules us: "Thou shalt love the Lord thy God with thy whole heart and with thy whole soul and with thy whole mind" (Mt. 22:37). Padre Pio wanted a pure and complete faithfulness to God. Faith and morality are the two-rail track of the Christian life. One must accept all the truths of the Christian faith and keep all the laws that the Gospel teaches us. This is the only way the Christian life leads to its goal, which is the kingdom of heaven.

Catholics who are convinced, who practice their faith, who give good example, Catholics completely of one piece ("d'un pezzo"), that is, solid Catholics —that is the way Padre Pio wanted his spiritual children and his penitents to be. In matters of faith and morals he allowed no ambiguity or compromise.

When someone spoke well of the non-Catholic abbey of Taizé, or told of experiences with other churches or religions, Padre Pio used to respond clearly and firmly:

"They have only a part of the light. We have the full light."

Once some men indicated to him that they considered themselves both Catholics and Communists. Padre Pio remarked in a pained voice, "Catholic Communists! Can greater nonsense than that be uttered?" When people spoke of some modern trends that are destroying faith, he seemed to suffer like a man afflicted with a crushing grief. When people talked to him about the thinking of the modernist theologians who subtly attack fundamental truths of faith, such as Christ's Resurrection, His divinity, Mary's virginal maternity, the existence of hell, etc., and asked his advice on how to re-act, they always heard a pained answer uttered loudly and assuringly: "These teachings cannot change as long as the Holy Spirit does not change."

Some days before his death, when a spiritual daughter greeted Padre Pio, he put his hand on her head and twice said to her forcefully, "Daughter, be constant and persevering in the faith of our fathers."

Once a bishop spoke to him about the spiritual and moral ruin resulting from rebelliousness among the clergy, and was reporting the tragic scandals seen in

the pulpit and in the use of the sacraments. Interrupting, Padre Pio said with great sorrow, "That is adequate ... Do not cut my heart!"

A fellow friar who was a Scripture professor was praising the studies of modernist interpreters of the Bible. Padre Pio responded sadly and dryly, "What an achievement! You have taken away the words of God and given us the words of poor men."

A higher superior in the Franciscan Order went to speak to him about the modern renewal within the Order and the new Constitutions. Padre Pio pointed his finger at him and said, "Do not change the nature of our Order! Do not pervert things! One day, in the presence of God, St. Francis will not recognize you as his own."

People told him that some priests were teaching that one could go to holy Communion after a mortal sin as long as one had first said a simple act of sorrow, without first going to confession, and that some preachers said that there was no longer an obligation to attend Mass on Sunday, and were denying the value of prayer. Padre Pio used to respond to these accounts with tears, and would urge the frequent recitation of this ejaculation, "O Jesus, save the elect in the hour of darkness." He used to urge everybody —priests, religious, and simple faithful— to preserve a firm and untainted faithfulness to a God Who said, "I am the Lord and I change not" (Mal. 3:6).

A son of the Church

Padre Pio was always a very docile and devout son of the Church. One time, during a discussion of a religious nature when others were endeavoring to uphold new opinions of modern thinkers, Padre Pio abruptly interrupted everything with the remark, "You can say what you like, but I stand with the Church, and that is enough."

Padre Pio's life was a continual demonstration of his assertion, "I stand by the Church." He described the Church as "our tender mother." How many times he offered himself entirely to be a victim, to be a sacrifice for her needs!

It was especially during his final years that Padre Pio suffered anguish over the division and rebelliousness within the Church. His one consolation was in a future not far away, as he said, when the Church would be rebuilt as "one fold under one Shepherd" (John 10:16).

He gave his greatest proof of love for the Church during the harsh trials to which he was subjected. His behavior during the ten long years of suffering was one of heroic obedience in silence and humility. When he was under the lash, so to speak, he had it in him to say, "Sweet is the hand of the Church, even when she strikes, for it is the hand of one's mother." And of all the young insubordinate clergy and religious who made the

Church suffer, he used to say that "they have no brains and no heart." We know the great respect and devotion with which he accepted the dispositions of the Holy See of Rome, even when they were against him. There were several times during half a century when the Father Superior had to enter Padre Pio's room to read a letter or document to him from the Church authorities which imposed severe measures upon him. Padre Pio would rise to his feet at once, listen with his head bowed, and at the end say, "I thank God!"

Later he would weep and pray.

The noblest and greatest gesture that Padre Pio made towards the Church was that of leaving his whole work in her hands, willing it to the Holy See. One day, speaking of the Home for the Relief of Suffering, he confided to a spiritual son,

"Notice that I made a will leaving everything to the Church; for I am a son of the Church. And when I no longer manage anything, my Mother will have to answer for all the offerings, even the coins, that souls from all over the world donate to the Home for the Relief of Suffering. I have done this as a sacred duty in order to see that there would be no interference."

He had a special reverence for the Pope. He always kept a photograph of the Pope in his room, and at night the little light that shone on his little Madonna image, also shone on the Pope's picture.

When the Bishop of Manfredonia was going to visit the Pope, Padre Pio said to him,

"Tell the Pope that for me, after Jesus, there is no one but him."

He often exhorted people to pray for the Pope, "whom I love in my love for Jesus." When he learned that Pius XII was ill, he sent good wishes to him through Prof. Enrico Medi, to whom he said,

"Tell the Pope that I gladly offer my life for him."

During Pope John XXIII's last agony, Padre Pio was seen spending a very long time praying for him. We know the great veneration he had for the Pope's teaching office, the importance he attached to instructions of Pius XII and his zeal not to let papal exhortations and directives go neglected.

Before his death, Padre Pio wrote his last letter on this earth

He wrote a letter to Pope Paul VI. It was the final action of a devoted son in behalf of his mother the Church. It conveyed his affection and gratitude. It expressed his generous offer of his life for the Church, and his confident hopes for her future. The letter was a great comfort to the heart of the Pope and a great example for all of us children of the Church.

Defender of life

One thing above all that Padre Pio took to heart was the defense of life and of the wellsprings of life. The sin against life used to make him react with zeal and forcefulness.

The family, holy matrimony, chastity, found in him an unwavering defender. He required respect and attention for these realities that belong to God's plan for the increase of the human race. Padre Pio saved quite a number of families from breaking up and from divorce. He loudly proclaimed that divorce is "creation... destroyed by man," and thus it is "the main highway that leads to hell." And when divorce becomes part of civil law, the future of society itself is put in peril.

Padre Pio had a special place in his heart for the numerous family. He said that "matrimony is for children," and, as holy Scripture reads, "Children are a gift of the Lord" (Ps. 126:3).

The good wishes he was accustomed to give newlyweds was that their marriage be "beautifully crowned with children," in order to "populate the earth and paradise." From couples under his spiritual direction there sprung many numerous families with ten or more children.

He was unflinching in his condemnation of the birth control pill, which he considered a product of hell. His

position was the same against every abuse of marriage, which he saw as a wicked degradation of a sacred design.

Declining absolution, he energetically refused to tolerate anyone who clung to his sin and who of set purpose spurned the begetting of children. One day he said to someone, "May the Lord's vengeance not fall upon you." He admonished someone else: "When you married, God made the decision of how many children He ought to give you.":

Many raised objections about the burden of children. "When you have faith," Padre Pio answered, "children do not overburden your health, nor your finances, nor your nerves." Once at a gathering of men who were talking, Padre Pio pointed out a gentleman who was walking up to them, a Professor Manelli, and he said softly to those present, "That gentleman lives fully by the Gospel... I am obliged to blush before him."

The gentleman was the father of twenty-one children. It was this family that Padre Pio called "my family." Therefore Padre Pio greatly rejoiced when the encyclical *Humanae vitae* was issued, which re-affirmed the Church's teaching on the matter of family limitation. In a letter he wrote shortly before his death, Padre Pio expressly thanked the Pope for this encyclical.

Padre Pio was immovable in his stand against all sins of impurity, whether committed alone or with others. As the Church has always taught, these sins pro-

fane the wellsprings of life and provoke God's high displeasure. Quite often Padre Pio, for their own good, refused absolution to persons guilty of these sins, exclaiming to them, "Do not defile yourself!"

A special chapter would be required if we would tell the story of Padre Pio's fight against immodest fashions. He expected women to dress with the modesty that one looks for in God-fearing persons. "Go get dressed!" Oh, how often Padre Pio exclaimed those words! Once he said to a woman penitent, "I would saw off those arms if I were you; for then you would suffer less than you will otherwise suffer in Purgatory. Naked parts of your body will burn."

Still greater was Padre Pio's war on other very grave evils, such as homosexuality, euthanasia, and abortion. He regarded these sins as the great abomination of mankind and the destruction of all Christian and human values.

The Home for the Relief of Suffering (Casa Sollievo della Sofferenza)

A great medical center alongside the Shrine of Santa Maria delle Grazie at San Giovanni Rotondo got its start during the evening of January 9, 1940. Padre Pio shared his joy with three of his spiritual sons —the pharmacist Charles Kisvarday, the physician William

Sanguinetti, and a farmer named Mario Sanvico. He told them, "My great project that belongs to this world was launched this evening." He held in his hand the first contribution, a gold coin worth ten francs— nothing else. It was the gift of an unidentified elderly lady.

Considering the time and place, it might have appeared to be a foolhardy project. It was during the war, and it was in a rugged, out-of-the way location. But great is the faith of the saints. The collection of offerings began at once, and they were not slow to come in from all parts of the world.

In May 1947 construction began, and in nine years the hospital complex was completed. On May 5, 1956, the inauguration of the Home for the Relief of Suffering, the *Casa Sollievo*, took place. A blessing was given by Cardinal Giacomo Lercaro and a discourse of Pius XII was broadcast from Rome. From that time on, the Casa Sollievo has received an ever-growing number of the suffering members of the Mystical Body of Christ. It will always keep going, whatever storms may come. Padre Pio was sure of this when he said, "The Casa Sollievo is something God sustains with His own Hand. It is God's work and will go on during the centuries to come. Woe to the one who touches it!"

According to Padre Pio, the characteristic of the Casa ought to be this: "A place of prayer and of science." Faith and technology, Christian self-denial and

medical skill, mystical and medical realities, must "address themselves to the complete person, body and soul," as Pope Pius XII said in the discourse for the inauguration. For Padre Pio, the Casa Sollievo ought to be a "hospital community, technically sufficient to serve the most challenging clinical needs," but above all it had to be the place "where mankind would find itself in Christ crucified as one flock under one shepherd."

An objection was put to Padre Pio by certain persons: "Why make the Casa Sollievo so beautiful and attractive, so as to appear sumptuous?"

"Sumptuous?" Padre Pio responded. "If it were possible I would make the Casa of gold, for the patient served is Jesus, and everything that is done for the Lord is but little."

On another occasion Padre Pio said to those responsible for the labor, "Make it beautiful, like paradise; for Jesus is to come and be a patient."

For Padre Pio, in caring for the sick the right rank of values must be respected —first there is God's grace; then there is man's activity. This was the supernatural technique of St. Joseph Moscati, the noted physician of Naples. Becoming but an echo of St. Moscatti, Padre Pio once addressed these words to a symposium that included noted physicians from all parts of the world gathered at San Giovanni Rotondo: "Your mission is to care for the sick. But if you bring no love to the sick-

bed, I do not believe that the medicines will help much. I have tested this... Bring God to the sick; it will be worth more than any other care you give..."

The Home for the Relief of Suffering will be a perpetual witness of the fruitfulness of God's love. God's love is showered on his creatures. Whoever is filled with love for God cannot fail to give himself to others. This is the way all the Saints became Saints.

The love of Jesus spurred on Padre Pio to give himself for his sick fellowmen, both those ailing in soul and those ailing in body.

To care for spiritual sickness, he dedicated his whole self to the priestly ministry of confession and spiritual direction. To care for bodily sickness he wanted to establish a hospital which would not be a place where only grief and pain would be the normal thing to see, but he wanted it to be a home that would be lovely and peaceful, where one would find relief from suffering.

Prayer Groups

"Prayer groups" were also a work of Padre Pio. At present there are very many of these, and they constitute a live force within the Church, bearing a message that is fully that of the Gospel and carrying the seal of approval of the life of a priest crucified for fifty years.

On September 24, 1975, the Padre Pio Prayer Groups were granted a papal audience, and the Holy Father Paul VI spoke of "Padre Pio of Pietrelcina who, among his many great and worthy achievements, gave birth to this army, this stream of people who pray, and who, by their example and their trust in spiritual aid, dedicate themselves to the Christian life and give witness of a sharing in prayer, in charity, in poverty of spirit, and in zeal for the Christian life."

A "stream of people who pray...and give witness... in zeal for the Christian life"— such are the Padre Pio Prayer Groups. They must be a Christianity that prays, that is alive, that is active. Then they will be "beacons shedding light and love in the world," as Padre Pio said, amid the darkness of error and violence and "the confusion of ideas" that is bringing havoc to society and the Church. These Groups were a prophetic institution, inspired on the occasion of an exhortation of Pope Pius XII. Padre Pio made its message his own and fulfilled it like an attentive and docile son of the Vicar of Christ. "Let us set about the task," Padre Pio said at the time, "and let us roll up our sleeves. Let us be the first to answer this appeal given by the Roman Pontiff."

Many years previously, in 1914, Padre Pio had traced a sketch of a magnificent program of Prayer Groups in a letter to a spiritual daughter. He told her that the Prayer Groups should be a witness to the world

and in the world of a "truly Christian" life nourished by "ceaseless prayer" so as to realize the essential contents of the Our Father.

The essential goals which the Prayer Groups set before themselves— including the glory of God, the salvation of sinners, the sanctification of souls— correspond to the fundamental aims of prayer itself; namely, adoration and praise, thanksgiving, propitiation, reparation. Padre Pio often repeated, "What is lacking in man is prayer."

And it is true. If things are taking an evil course, if our society is harassed by so much violence and corruption, it is because it has lost the life-giving and saving contact with Him Who said, "He who follows Me does not walk in darkness" (John 8:12).

It is a simple procedure to set up a Padre Pio Prayer Group. One can do it with just a few members. It is enough to find a priest who is willing to direct the Group, and have the Bishop's blessing. For Padre Pio said, "Do nothing without the consent and permission of the Bishops and the priests. Do all with a common accord, and be obedient."

Thus one or more gatherings for prayer are organized for each month. It is well that each gathering not omit the holy Rosary and a meditation such as the message and example of Padre Pio would inspire. If members of a Group are faithful, they will attract oth-

ers and truly become a "beacon shedding light and love in the world." One day before God they will comprehend the great value and vital need of this life of prayer which the Prayer Groups are called to fulfill.

"This is the highest apostolate that a soul can exercise in the Church," Padre Pio assures us.

Jubilarian

No one else has been able to celebrate the completion of such an amazing half century as Padre Pio has —fifty years of the stigmata; that is, fifty years of wounds and blood, of fever and piercing pains. As for the stigmatized Saints we know about, the duration of their stigmata was much shorter. These persons include St. Francis of Assisi, St. Veronica Giuliani, St. Gemma Galgani— all were crucified victims consumed in a brief time by the "consuming fire" (Deut.4:24) of love for God. But Padre Pio for a full half century had the mission of showing the world a likeness, a conformity to the crucified Jesus. It was a unique and disconcerting witness to the truth of those great words of St. Paul, "I bear the marks of the Lord Jesus in my body" (Gal. 6:17), "that the life also of Jesus may be made manifest in our mortal flesh" (II Cor. 4: 11).

On the morning of September 20, 1968, at San Giovanni Rotondo there was an atmosphere of festivity

and extraordinary rejoicing. People from all parts of Italy and the world made up a countless throng. Thousands of busses parked along the streets and in the public squares of the town. Crowds bustled everywhere— in the church, the restaurants, the hotels, the homes, and on the streets. Padre Pio celebrated Mass at his customary hour before a large crowd attentively and devoutly participating. A dense group of priests and religious were about the altar, while Padre Pio, slowly and painfully, renewed the sacrifice of Christ, in which, by means of the stigmata, he was made to share the pains of his crucified Savior.

It was his last Mass but for one more. The altar, the sanctuary, the choir loft were decorated with red flowers —fifty vases of red roses for fifty years of blood. Immediately after the Mass, Padre Pio, looking handsome, as his face shone with a paternal sweetness, passed through two long rows of priests who were there to honor him with filial affection. Then he entered the confessional as usual. Never a respite, not even on this exceptional day!

Toward nightfall, in honor of Padre Pio, a candlelight procession marched up from the town and there was a display of fireworks. But Padre Pio was feeling ill. He could not even make an appearance. His little window remained shut. The next morning he was unable to celebrate Mass.

Fifty years of blood! "My whole life," Padre Pio once wrote, "is a passage from the altar of sacrifice to the altar of holocaust." That is, throughout his priestly life he offered himself to be a victim with Christ, and God repeatedly sacrificed him as a willing victim with Christ. An amazing fifty years! One cannot live a half century with five wounds shedding blood every day, without a special gift from God.

Fifty years of grace! By means of Padre Pio countless souls obtained conversion and salvation, and very many others with physical ailments have been healed or helped.

Victimhood completed

Padre Pio died repeating up to the last moment the names he loved: "Jesus, Mary— Jesus, Mary."

It happened this way: Sunday morning, September 22, 1968, an immense crowd gathered at San Giovanni Rotondo once more. There was an international meeting of Padre Pio Prayer Groups. Padre Pio was able to celebrate holy Mass that morning, and the Father Superior asked him to do the favor of singing the Mass. Padre Pio was nearing his end. All perceived that he was worn out. He sang the Mass, but he seemed to sing from up on the Cross. His deep voice was hoarse, labored, and painful to listen to.

Finally at the end of the Mass Padre Pio had a collapse. He would have fallen if some nearby friars had not grabbed him in time.

Voices of alarm rose from the people as they saw him tottering. He still had the strength to repeat in a fatherly tone, "My children, my children..." It was the sign of his approaching end, though no one wanted to think so. For his spiritual children, Padre Pio's time to die would be —who knows when?— who knows but that he would reach a hundred?

That same morning Padre Pio, weak as he was, wanted to go down to hear the confessions of a small group. When that was finished he had himself carried to the choir window, from which he greeted the Prayer Group members attending their international meeting.

There were two other very significant events that same day, namely, the blessing of the crypt of the new church, and the laying of the first stone of a monumental Way of the Cross, which Padre Pio's spiritual sons and daughters were offering him on the occasion of the fiftieth year of his stigmata. Who would ever have thought that the crypt would soon serve as Padre Pio's burying place?[11] It was blessed just in time.

As for the Way of the Cross, his spiritual sons and daughters could not have thought of a gift more agreeable to a man whose body bore "the marks of the Lord Jesus." Significantly, wherever Simon the Cyrenean

appears in these depictions, the sculptor has given him the features and habit of Padre Pio. Thus, on the side of the mountain a sculptured reminder remains of Padre Pio's fifty years with Christ's wounds, another Cyrenean bearing the Cross after Jesus and "become like to Him in death" (Phil. 3:10).

That evening people were relieved to see Padre Pio at the Eucharist devotions. He was in the gallery, Rosary beads in hand. At the close of the function he stood for a while, supported by some friars, taking his last look at the church full of people.

Then he withdrew to his room. When someone asked how he felt, he answered, "Bad, bad, my son. The only thing I lack is a grave. I am more in the grave than here."

After midnight he asked the friar that was with him to celebrate Mass for him in the morning. Then he went to confession. He urged the friar to ask the pardon of the other friars for the disturbances he had caused. From everyone— friars and his spiritual children— he begged a prayer for his soul and he assured everyone of his blessing— his fellow friars, his spiritual sons and daughters, his hospital patients.

He renewed his religious profession as a Capuchin, and said the Our Father in a clear voice. Then he rose, and, dressed as always in the garb of St. Francis, he moved surprisingly fast, "like a young man," left his

room, went out on the terrace, and stood there a few minutes. Then he was carried back indoors, and rested in an armchair. He gazed at the wall where there was a picture of his mother, and said, "I see two mothers."

The friar told him he was not seeing well, because there was only the one picture of his mother. But Padre Pio responded, "Do not worry. I see very well. I see two mothers there."

Padre Pio began to turn pale. Perspiration formed beads on his forehead. His lips were livid as he repeated, "Jesus, Mary— Jesus, Mary!"

It was two A.M. The friar attending him realized that things were happening fast and was about to run for help. Padre Pio stopped him twice, "Do not wake anybody up."

The friar hastened off nevertheless. Then the Father Superior, some other friars, and a physician arrived. After awhile other friars and physicians came.

Padre Pio received the anointing of the sick. His lips barely moved as he kept repeating, "Jesus, Mary, Jesus, Mary!"

It was the end. His head bowed over his breast and he breathed no more. He had passed into eternity.

Those present stood recollected in their thoughts and prayers for a long while, almost petrified with grief. Then their feelings were released. They could not hold back the tears.

Meantime outside the friary Padre Pio's spiritual sons and daughters kept watch, and with anxious fears awaited the dawn to learn the news. In the morning the terrible news quickly spread: "Padre Pio is dead! God has taken his soul."

The sad news had been unhappily foreseen. Everywhere the evidence of grief was indescribable. All through the throng that filled the church and the square in front of it one saw faces stricken with sorrow, men weeping like babies. Most of the people were holding their Rosaries without seeming able to pray. There was a great void in everyone's heart, as if their own father or mother had passed away.

The secret of the King

Immediately after Padre Pio's death something astonishing was discovered about his body. The five stigmata had totally disappeared. The flesh was once more intact, the skin appearing as uniform and smooth as that of an infant.

Padre Pio's prayer to obtain the removal of these outward signs of the Savior's sufferings, was finally heard. Who knows what scientific studies men might have wanted to make on the mystery of those wounds. But the "secret of the King" (Tobias 12:7) remained with God, to our confusion.

It is true that for some time the bleeding of Padre Pio's stigmata had started diminishing, and lately no blood clot appeared on the palms or backs of his hands. But the total disappearance of every scar evokes the conclusion, "This is the finger of God" (Ex. 8:19).

We venture to propose a beautiful and precious significance to this event; that is, the slow decrease in the bleeding was to indicate that Padre Pio's mission was reaching its end; that the victim had arrived at the completion of the sacrifice, drained of his blood, like Jesus on the Cross.

May all honor and glory be given to God, Who in our days has chosen to show His power and His love in this creature in whom He impressed "the sign of the living God" Apoc. 7:2).

Greater than when alive

Padre Pio's funeral was four days after his death. The procession seemed endless. People had come from all parts of the world to honor the remains of the remarkable Capuchin. According to estimates, about a hundred thousand persons had come for the funeral. The function was marked with a deeply moving nobility. In the blue sky overhead squadrons of aircraft moved in formation to escort the procession, which extended nearly five miles.

The Casa Sollievo was decked with the flags of various nations at half-mast. For about three hours Professor Enrico Medi stood at the microphone as commentator and leader in the reflections on the mysteries of the Rosary. The function seemed more like a solemn homage to a Saint than a funeral procession.

The holy Mass and the blessing of the remains took place in the square in front of the shrine. The whole ceremony was marked with majestic solemnity and devotion.

Patients in the Casa Sollievo followed the rites from the hospital windows and at nightfall powerful outdoor floodlights were put in operation that shone upon the Casa Sollievo and the shrine church.

It was a great tribute to Padre Pio, to his projects, and to his spiritual sons and daughters.

Nevertheless, after Padre Pio's death, some had serious worries as to whether the great and beautiful projects that he had started and developed, would continue. Some people were quite sure that the shrine would greatly decline, that hotels and restaurants would stop operating, that the flow of pilgrims would dwindle and that the hospital would have a difficult time. Instead just the opposite happened. Padre Pio had said some years before,

"I will make more noise when I am dead than when I was live."

Also, "In paradise I will work with both hands." And in fact from the time of his death onwards, the development of San Giovanni Rotondo has been a spectacle before the world and a marvel to all observers. Pilgrims continue to flock to the shrine; the Casa Sollievo has been enlarged; the hotels and restaurants thrive. Newly completed are the impressive, extensive Via Crucis, the Rosary Park ("Piazzale del Rosario"), the Padre Pio Art Center ("Centro Artistico Padre Pio").

Padre Pio's writings have been published; the fame of his miracles continues to spread; new houses and buildings continue to rise in the area; the Prayer Group organization holds meetings on both national and international levels. All this, and more, has happened after Padre Pio's death. This continuing activity shows a deep-rooted, fruitful vitality that will not wane, for it is rooted in Padre Pio's heart and blood, in his virtues and his wounds.

Toward the Honors of the Altar

Immediately following Padre Pio's death steps were taken toward opening the process for his beatification and canonization.

It is true that many faithful followers of Padre Pio, who number millions and millions, would have wanted and would like to have Padre Pio immediately declared

a Saint. In their hearts they already consider him one. "The voice of the people, the voice of God," runs the proverb. But the Church's way requires stages. One step at a time, and one will arrive at the desired day.

Pope John Paul II's visit to San Giovanni Rotondo in 1987 to mark the hundredth anniversary of Padre Pio's birth was deeply significant.

And then, on December 21, 1998, it was announced by Joaquin Navarro-Valls, Director of the Holy See's Press Office, that "The ceremony for the beatification of Servant of God Pio da Pietrelcina is scheduled for May 2, 1999."

And so it came to pass, with untold thousands, even millions, present to do honor to this child of Mary honored by the Savior.

"He who attaches himself to the earth remains attached to it. It is by violence that we must leave it. It is better to detach oneself a little at a time, rather than all at once. Let us always think of Heaven".

Endnotes

[1] This book is translated from the author's *Padre Pio da Pietrelcina*, an Italian paperback of 189 pages in a revised edition published "*con approvazione ecclesiastica*" by Casa Mariana, 83040 Frigento (AV), Italy, in 1995. The author's work is prefaced with this declaration (in Italian): "In obedience to the decree of Pope Urban VIII we attribute no more than human faith to any extraordinary facts narrated in this book and we intend to abide by the definitive judgment of the Church." Insofar as a priest in some way represents the Church, the author must qualify with this declaration his reports of extraordinary facts like many here published, regardless of how sure he feels of what he says—at least until the authorities of the Church have finished their investigation and pronounced a favorable judgment.

[2] St. Pellegrino of Alpi was an eighth century Scotch prince who refused the throne, gave his property to the poor, and made pilgrimages to shrines, including St. Michael's on Mt. Gargano, Italy, where he became well-known.

[3] Grazio Forgione, a native of Pietrelcina, was a humble farmer. He went to America twice to find work for the support of his family. He spent his last years at San Giovanni Rotondo, Italy, and died on October 7, 1946, at the age of 86, assisted by his son.

Maria Giuseppa di Nunzio, known familiarly as Mamma Peppa, was also born at Pietrelcina. She was a good, energetic woman, richly endowed with faith. Her concern was to bring up her children in the fear of the Lord, and her efforts were bountifully rewarded. She died at 70, also assisted by her son, who held her in great affection.

[4] In discerning a divine vision, revelation, miracle, an important observation is that any devil, in producing his prodigies, aims at causing *formal* (culpable) sin, not purely material sin (blameless due to incul-

pable error), because he wants us to truly insult God, which purely material sin does not do. And so one may expect the devil to want there to be some clue that his prodigies are NOT divine signs of ways to please God. Thus all could compare the power of Pharao's satanic magicians with the power of God's prodigies worked through Moses, His spokesman (Exodus chapters 5-12, 14). Do not some people today find in today's diabolical phenomena an excuse to conclude: "We need not heed prodigies of Fatima, Lourdes, Tre Fontane, or those of Padre Pio and Saints, for we can never know which prodigies are from God, if any, and which are from other spirits"? Not being supremely interested in pleasing and detecting orders from the Mightiest Master, they can easily become no more interested in distinguishing between prodigy and prodigy than Pharao was, or certain wicked Jewish leaders were, who bribed wicked soldiers to spread a lie that the Apostles had stolen Our Lord's Body, which had risen (Mt. 28:11-15).

[5] "Io mi lamentai con lui perché si era fatto così lungamente aspettare, mentre non avevo mancato di chimarlo in mio soccorso. Quasi per punirlo del ritardo, non volevo neppure guardarlo in viso, volevo allontanarmi; ma egli poverino mi raggiunse quasi piangendo, mi prese finché sollevato lo sguardo, lo fissai in volto e lo trovai tutto spiacente."

[6] Don Nello Castello, *Gesù Crocifisso in Padre Pio,* pp. 76-78 (Casa Mariana, Frigento AV, Italy).

[7] The late Professor Manelli was father of the author.

[8] Documentation and details of Padre Pio's countless miracles are given by Francobaldo Chiocci and Luciano Cirri in *Padre Pio: Storia d'una Vittima,* published in three volumes in 1967 in Rome. For Gemma's wonderful case see vol. 1, pp. 660-666, and vol. 3, p. 229; also Nesta de Robeck's *Padre Pio* (Milwaukee, USA, 1959) and Fernando da Riese Pio Decimo's *Padre Pio da Pieltrelcina* (Rome: Postulazione Generale Cappuccini, 1975), pp. 332-333.

[9] This modern hospital and medical center began functioning on May 5, 1956. Its construction was made possible by offerings of Padre Pio's spiritual children from all over the world. "This is all a work of Providence," said Padre Pio on the day it opened its doors.

[10] The writer Alberto del Fante has written an excellent book entitled *Per la Storia: Padre Pio di Pietrelcina, Il Primo Sacerdote Stigmatizzato, e Fatti Nuovi* (S. Giovanni Rotondo, Foggia , Italy: Editrice Libreria S. Maria delle Grazie, 1969). Besides presenting a beautiful account of his own conversion, he presents dozens of impressive accounts of how others likewise gained or regained the Catholic Faith and divine grace through the help of Padre Pio. He confirms many of these accounts with excerpts from letters and statements of witnesses, especially the converts themselves. Typical is a letter from an ex-mason of Bologna, Ferruccio Caponetti, who tells how he presented to Padre Pio his objections to the faith and how the Capuchin stigmatic, "with simple language but with great depth of thought, demolished one by one all the theories of which my mind was full, so that I had no argument to put forth. He laid my soul bare, and having shown me the lofty teaching of Our Lord, he re-opened the eyes of my spirit. I saw the true light. He reached my heart, and I knew the true faith." (P. 232) Del Fante also presents good accounts of dozens of Padre Pio's miracles, confirming many of these with excerpts from letters and statements.

[11] The new church, built alongside the old friary church, was consecrated on July 1, 1959. In the crypt beneath the church is Padre Pio's tomb, a perpetual place of pilgrimages from all over the world.

APPENDIX (by the Translator)

The Miracle of the Stigmata

Jesuit Fr. John A. Hardon's *Pocket Catholic Dictionary* (New York, Doubleday, 1985: ISBN 0-385-23238-1), under "Stigmata" writes that the stigmata are a phenomenon "in which a person bears all or some of the wounds of Christ in his or her own body, i.e., on the feet, hands, side, and brow. The wounds appear spontaneously, from no external source, and periodically there is a flow of fresh blood. The best known stigmatic (that is, one who bore the stigmata) was St. Francis of Assisi... Authentic stigmatization occurs only among people favored with ecstasy and is preceded and attended by keen physical and moral sufferings that thus make the subject conformable to the suffering Christ." Certain critics who admit the reality of the phenomenon have called this suffering masochism, implying that Catholic Saints who experienced it, desired in it and felt in it a perverted sexual delight. However we Catholics accepting the true doctrine admit indeed a certain non-sexual joy which Saints experience in this victimhood, to which victimhood they will have offered themselves, but we are convinced that this victimhood serves holy ends that Saints rightly want to serve. The Translator once presented to a misinformed non-Catholic critic this example by way of illustrating this Providence:— Envision a fond but ailing mother whose rising

from bed and tending her sick baby, doubles her backache and head pains, but out of love she *wants* to render this needed service to her baby, and her love for the child can put a kind of joy into her willing self-sacrifice. I asked this critic, "Would you call that mother's self-sacrifice masochism?" And the answer that came was, "Indeed not! It would be sublimation." Nor was it masochism that made St. John Vianney rejoice when, from praeternatural causes which God allowed, he underwent on certain nights terrible physical sufferings (which we think were from the devil); for he knew by experience that when these sufferings came, the next morning he would "catch a big fish," as he said, in the confessional. Some hardened sinner clearly heading for hell would be touched by divine grace, and the next morning come sincerely repentant to his confessional. On account of his love for God and souls, these conversions brought the Saint more than enough joy to make up for all he suffered. St. Francis of Assisi and other enlightened, holy stigmatics, knowing the Catholic doctrines on the matter, understood that their pains patiently borne in order to agree with God's mysterious designs, were God's instrument for many conversions, and so rejoiced in such suffering out of love for God's will which they wanted to see fulfilled, and out of love for souls. These holy persons' sufferings derived their value from our divine Savior's sufferings because, like St. Paul, such persons knew that their pains were to "fill up those things that are wanting of the sufferings of Christ... for His body, which is the Church" (Col. 1:24). Could one not call this sublimation on a supernatural level?

Blessed Padre Pio
The Wonder Worker

If there is such a thing as rivalry in heaven, Padre Pio would give the great Wonder Worker *(thaumaturgust)* St. Anthony of Padua stiff competition for that title. The new Blessed, Padre Pio is a 20th century version of the 13th century Saint. The many gifts Padre Pio had such as bilocation, miraculous scents, prophecy, reading hearts, healing, interpreting languages and many other charisms, ranks him among the most extraordinary Saints in the two-thousand year history of the Church.

This latest book in the *"Marian Shrines and Saints"* series, *Padre Pio — The Wonder Worker,* not only examines these gifts close up and from different perspectives but is capable of challenging the faithless, of exciting interest among the wavering and of inspiring the faithful to aspire to holiness.

The first seven chapters are a biographical sketch, followed by over thirty chapters dealing with the many inspiring facts pertaining to his life and charisms.

The book is well illustrated and should be a best seller similar to the other books of the series, *Marian Shrines and Saints.*

For further information: Academy of the Immaculate, POB 667, Valatie, NY 12184, phone and FAX (518) 758-1584, E-mail—Mimike@pipeline.com. or Friars of the Immaculate, P.O. Box 3003, New Bedford, MA 02741 (508) 984-1856, FAX (508) 996-8296, E-mail: ffi@marymediatrix.com

Suggested offering $9.50 (normally $12.95); 5 to 19 copies $8.00 plus PH; 20 or more $6.50 ea. plus PH;

EUCHARISTIC-MARIAN READING

Obviously there is a need for good, solid devotional books on Marian Shrines and Saints outstanding in their love for the Blessed Mother and the Eucharistic Jesus. The Franciscan Friars of the Immaculate are attempting to meet this need and flood the book market with readable inspirational books at a reasonable cost.

A Handbook on Guadalupe

The latest, authoritative book on Guadalupe covers the theme with 40 topical chapters, written by leading experts on Guadalupe. A treasure of facts and insights, with many new exciting discoveries, it contains the latest research by experts on Guadalupana from Mexico and the United States. There are over 50 illustrations (20 full color) in the Handbook's 244 pages, along with short chapters, makes for easy, enjoyable reading. ($12.50)*

St. Thérèse: Doctor of the Little Way

"Among the many books about St. Thèrèse, this one is unique because it offers a compendium of insights from 23 writers who have contributed chapters on all aspects of the life and spirituality of this new Doctor of the Church. Authors present topics such as: The Little Way of Thérèse, St. of the Eucharist, Thérèse's Use of Scripture, Abandonment through Suffering, Mirror of the Blessed Virgin and Mystical Simplicity." (Ignatius Press) The 174 page book has 36 illustrations, some never seen before. ($9.95)*

Jesus Our Eucharistic Love *by Fr. Stefano Manelli, F.I.*

This little treasure of Eucharistic devotion is based on the writing and examples taken from the lives of the Saints. It is bound to inspire a greater love and devotion to Jesus' presence in the Blessed Sacrament. Ideal for meditative reading before the Eucharist. "Although God is all-powerful, He is unable to give more: though su-

premely wise, He knows not how to give more: though vastly rich, He has not more to give." St. Augustine ($5.00)*

All Generations Shall Call Me Blessed *by Fr. Manelli, F.I.*
Fr. Stephano well known in Italy for his scholarly and popular writings, is the co-founder of the Franciscan Friars of the Immaculate. He traces Mary's role as the Woman of the Protoevangelium, through the Old Testament figures and symbols, into the New Testament where we see the many instances and places where Mary is found working beside her Divine Son. The clear and concise exposition of Mary as Virgin-Mother and Queen (all Biblical) is an ideal way of explaining her vital role in the economy of Salvation. ($19.95)*

Virgo facta Ecclesia *by Franciscans of the Immaculate*
The 174 page, two part book, a biography of St. Francis and the Mariological basis for the Franciscan Order: a digest of Mary Immaculate's place in the Franciscan Order from St. Francis to St. Maximilian. Some thought provoking subtitles: Mary Immaculate Magistra: Understanding the Franciscan Charism, Virgin Made Church: The Immaculate and the Purpose of Franciscanism, Transubstantiation into the Immaculate and Franciscan Profession of Vows: Perfect Conformity to Christ Crucified. ($5.00)*

Totus Tuus *by Msgr. Arthur Burton Calkins*
Monsignor Calkins is an official of the Pontifical Commission: "Ecclesia Dei" in Rome. This book examines issues of Marian consecration, historically and in the thoughts of the Holy Father, and why the Holy Father finds entrustment to Mary so vital in today's Church. *Totus Tuus* provides a thorough examination of the magisterial teaching especially that of John Paul II, theological and scriptural for total consecration to Mary. ($14.95)*

Not Made by Hands, *by Thomas Sennott*

This is the only book of its kind on the two most famous and controversial images in existence— the holy image of Our Lady of Guadalupe on the tilma of Bl. Juan Diego, and the scared image of the crucified Christ on the holy Shroud of Turin. Written by a scientist-religious, it is a good rebuttal of those who would say either of these images is a fraud. The fraudulent carbon fourteen test of 1998, which has been rejected by the prestigious scientific journal, *Science Today*, is answered by hard factual evidence to the contrary. Illustrated with many photos. ($ 7.95)*

You Will Make This Known, The Story of France's Three Major Shrines, *Edited by Bro. Francis Mary, FFI*

This book tells the exciting stories of Our Lady's appearances at Lourdes, La Salette and rue du Bac (Paris) in the 1800's, and the resulting three major Marian shrines in France. The title is taken from the departing words of Our Lady to the two children at La Salette: "You will make this known to all my people…" a stirring challenge to all Catholics to be evangelizers in response to Pope John Paul II's continual plea and Our Lady's request. Many color photos. ($12.95)*

*Prices here are suggested donations.

Special bulk rates from 10% to 60% depending on the number of books, plus postage.

For ordering books and further information on very attractive bulk rates: Academy of the Immaculate, POB 667, Valatie NY 12184, phone/FAX (518) 758-1584, E-mail: Mimike@pipeline.com.

Quotations on bulk rates shipped directly by the box contact: Friars of the Immaculate, POB 3003, New Bedford, MA 02740, (508) 984-1856, FAX (508) 996-8296, E-mail: ffi@marymediatrix.com

For the ones we don't know about

PREFACE

People always ask why you wrote this article or that book, and I suppose it is useful to try to answer, but in this case I have to say I am not sure. That is, I am not sure what it was about Ita Ford that resounded within me.

I can tell you that I found out about her when I read about her in *The New York Times* in early December, 1980, and realized that some fools in El Salvador had raped and killed four women missionaries, but that is not how I got to know Ita Ford.

I "met" her first through a Maryknoll publication—a small card with her photograph and a quote from her letter to her niece: "I hope you come to find that which gives life a deep meaning for you. Something worth living for— maybe even worth dying for...." Both the card and that sentiment stayed a long time with me, and when I was preparing *Woman to Woman: An Anthology of Women's Spiritualities* (The Liturgical Press, 1993) I went to the Maryknoll Archives to learn more about Ita Ford.

There is no preparation for encountering such a soul. I learned, and I continue to learn, about a genuinely good woman who truly lived as best she was able the life God laid out for her. Not all of it was her choice; not all of it was happy. All of it was lived joyfully in God's care.

I am still learning about Ita Ford; I want to write more about her. At this point, I can thank and thank deeply those who have shared both their time and their memories and,

1

while she would never impose such an order (or any order) on her many friends and relatives and acquaintances, those whom I have met so far here stand alphabetically side by side: Madeline Dorsey, MM, William P. Ford, Harry Gaffney, Kate Monahan Gregg, M. Edmund Harvey, RSHM, Peggy Healy, Mary Lou Herlihy, MM, Camilla Kennedy, MM, Grace Krieger, MM, Alfonse Ligouri, Beverly Malone, Janice McLaughlin, MM, Anna Mammana May, Grace Myerjack, MM, Grace Monahan Niemeyer, and Rose Tocci.

Thanks go as well to those who helped with research and translation: past and present staff of the Boston University Libraries and of the Maryknoll Archives, and Ana Ballester, Rene Duran, Antonio de las Morenas, M.D., Grace Krieger, MM, Brinsley Horner, Lorette Larkin, CSJ, Janice McLaughlin, MM, Virginia McKenna, RSHM, Phillip Redman, Teresa Rorke, CSJ, Raphael Velasquez, and Elizabeth Yakel;

to those who helped with final editing: James A. Brann and Kate Monahan Gregg;

to those whose research I used in the Maryknoll Archives: Judith Noone, MM, and Maureen Flanagan;

to those friends who walked with me as I began to walk with Ita, including Irene Kelly, RSHM, and Carolyn O'Hara, OCD;

and to Kathleen Walsh at Paulist Press.

All have helped me to correct my mistakes, and only I may have neglected to do so.

New York, October 18, 1995

I truly believe that I should be here and I can't even tell you why....God's palpable presence has never been more real ever since we came to Salvador—He's made a lot of things clear to us—what we should be doing, etc.—and I trust in that and I hope you can too.

—Ita Ford, September 7, 1980

INTRODUCTION

This life ended with a bullet in the brain.

At approximately 10:30 p.m. on December 2, 1980, Maryknoll Sister Ita Ford, having been abducted, stripped and brutalized, was shot in the back of the head by one of the following men: Luis Antonio Colindres Aleman, 25; Carlos Joaquin Contreras Palacios, 23; Francisco Orlando Contreras Recinos, 31; Jose Roberto Moreno Canjura, 24; Daniel Canales Ramirez, 23.

She was in El Salvador with three other American missionaries: Ursuline Sister Dorothy Kazel, Maryknoll Sister Maura Clarke, and Jean Donovan. Each was shot, and left uncovered and undressed. They were buried the next day in a common grave by local farmers.

Carlos Joaquin Contreras Palacios, the youngest, confessed. He tried later to explain that the women disrobed and submitted voluntarily, and that they had subversive propaganda with them. He, like the others, was a member of the Salvadoran National Guard.

These are the facts of the deaths. This is about Ita Ford's life.

I.

middle-class

It was cool and cloudy when Ita Ford was born in Brooklyn, on April 23, 1940. Her parents, Mildred Teresa O'Beirne and William Patrick Ford, had been born in this century to the promise of middle-class American life: she became the sort of New York City public school teacher who could "teach a carrot to read," he the genteel insurance agent, full of Irish song and wit.

Ita's brother, Bill, preceded her; her sister, Rene, came after. Together they endured "a Board of Education diet— wheat germ on everything" along with the usual constellation of big brother–middle sister–little sister consternations. Ita was always small—sometimes slight, sometimes chubby—by high school about 5'2" with the sort of build that causes yearbook editors to write "pixie" as part of the description. All her schooling was the white-glove Catholic of the 1950s and 1960s: Visitation Academy and The Fontbonne Hall Academy in Bay Ridge. Ita was assistant editor of her high school paper, editor of her college yearbook. At twenty-one she received a baccalaureate degree in English from Marymount Manhattan College, a small, Catholic commuter school on New York's Upper East Side.

Well before that she began to dream of missionary life. Early in her sophomore year in college she first contacted the Maryknoll Sisters of St. Dominic in Ossining, New York. She wrote to her friend Jean Baumann: "I've acquired a preliminary questionnaire for Maryknoll & I expect to go

7

up there Christmas week to look the place over....I'm doing my level best to make this thing work for next September."

It did not. Medical tests (her father had had tuberculosis) and Maryknoll's own determinations delayed her. Not incidentally, her mother remained unconvinced. Ita kept trying and found herself third time lucky, finally accepted for entrance in 1961. In the meanwhile, she had matured to "a new set of values" recognized after a senior-year trip to Russia: "It was the idea that these people...who really deserved freedom of religion—they were the ones denied it. It was pathetic and nauseating at the same time...[and] made me aware now that I really have to go to Maryknoll."

II.

Ita Catherine Ford entered Maryknoll in August, 1961, one of sixty-four young women endeavoring to learn missionary life. A postulant mistress of the time recalls her as "sophisticated"—a graduate of a "special" college, a gifted and acute observer who raised questions to the point of challenge. While Ita was not ordinarily allowed home visits, the postulant mistress remembers traveling with her on the New York subways heading for a family funeral in Brooklyn. With an eye for detail and a delight in the city around her, Ita pointed out the unique mosaics for each station—the beavers at Astor Place, for example—to the St. Louis native who accompanied her.

But her entry into religious life was difficult in many ways. She wrote: "It's lonely. Not in [the] sense of being alone in a crowd, but in an emotional way. No one knows you well enough to be able to say the right thing when you need it—and as yet, no one cares enough." The pain of separation waned as friendships formed, and her detachment from things material (but not from things intellectual) grew as the first year went on. She complained about the classes, and feared intellectual stagnation. In another letter she wrote: "...now I really don't mind having few belongings—it simplifies things—in fact I never thought a 3rd pair of shoes could be superfluous—now yes!"

A healthy detachment, and a deep understanding of what is known as poverty of spirit, are basic to religious life, and the process of letting go is lifelong. "Making" the stations of the cross, by meditating on the fourteen final events in the life and death of Jesus, often brings one to these points. Ita wrote her friend: "I'm not much of a station maker but one day during Lent I was thinking about it—and I was particularly struck by the tenth one. What could be harder than being stripped not of your clothes—but of all that goes to make you up, and yet what was more necessary than that very thing? Somehow you have to peel off all the layers you've acquired, all those things that go to hinder you when you really want to make the break. It fascinated me. I could see so many things that had to go—and still have to, if I was to get anywhere."

III.

The "stripping" required for a mature interior life should be a carefully monitored process. Maryknoll's novitiate, like others, could have added its own bureaucracy to the confusing time of preparation and of trial. Ita was never a fan of bureaucracy in any form; she wrote: "If anything could ruin your life, it's the petty daily stupidities—that so distract you from the all important."

Her early years at Maryknoll could not have been easy. She was a little older than the others, although by far not the eldest. She was more educated than most, and so she found the classes repetitive; she ached for copies of *The New Yorker* and almost anything else that would have stirred her literary mind. Her movement toward missionary life required a self-donation that the world generally does not understand, something she found hard to describe at first. She wrote about life within Maryknoll: "Even just to have a knowledge of the love that exists inside, and the reality of the relationship you can have with God....I am at a complete loss as how to explain this to anyone who thinks this is a waste of time."

She chafed at some things, excelled at others, and hung on. She was widely and well liked by the other novices. Still, the novitiate in Topsfield, Massachusetts became a pressure cooker for Ita. Another novice recalls that it seemed some were asked to leave suddenly, without reason or warning. The slips of paper in the mailboxes inevitably increased the tensions in the house, especially as the time for first vows drew near. Ita was worried—she wanted this so very much—and feared she would be the next to go. For whatever reason, she developed a "nervous stomach," and her initial medical evaluation could have blamed the stress of having to prove herself. Her first vows were temporarily delayed; she wrote to her friend: "My stomach has been on the skitz, and last Monday the doctor asked that I not be under the pressure of taking vows on the 24th."

The reprieve was short-lived, and the decision made final two months later: "I'm home—Wednesday afternoon it was official that I couldn't take vows....It's a shock and disappointment and I don't think I'm operating on all engines but I'll bounce soon."

IV.

There is a particular emotional danger for anyone asked to leave religious life, and the risk of imagining a "rejection by God" needs to be addressed quickly. However reluctantly religious orders might send someone away, a life's plan remains ruptured. While Ita's apparent physical condition would have ruled out her serving in foreign missions in the early 1960s (or today), Maryknoll was the only vocation she ever knew. Her dream was foreclosed in August, 1964, and she could not understand what happened, or why. She landed at LaGuardia bewildered, and went home to Brooklyn.

There was no hope of returning to Maryknoll, but there seems no embarrassment about her situation in her letters. Maryknoll had provided her with counseling before she left; she traveled to meet an additional six to eight times with the same woman psychiatrist until, as she put it, she decided she could have lunch a lot cheaper in New York than in Boston.

Ita also kept in touch with her truly compassionate novice mistress, Sister Paul Miriam: "It's four weeks since I arrived home, and though it's still very unreal, I am getting settled. Through Marymount I got a position at Sadlier Text Books, doing editorial work on a new series of High School English books. This is not completely new for I had been on the staff of the newspaper and yearbook. For right now it seems the best thing to do." She must have been encouraged to get involved with some sort of church work—she taught religious education classes part-time at a poor parish in lower Manhattan and reported back on her experiences: "Theoretically, I teach C.C.D., but I never teach any topic at all. They were supposed to be studying the commandments but they hardly know the basic prayers. Though Sunday mass isn't too high on their priority lists, they do have a wonderful Christian attitude toward each other. I guess that's why I love them."

V.

Ita continued to fall in love—with her friends, with her work, with her life, and with a young Japanese-American lawyer whom she perhaps thought she would marry.

She was an immediately likeable person, totally forthright and agreeable. When Harry Gaffney hired her at Sadlier she told him she left Maryknoll because she did not have the physical resources for missionary life. He recalls her as small but not sickly, one of many young, bright, articulate Catholics at the company. Sadlier's editorial department socialized a great deal, their closeness generated by an office layout that guaranteed constant contact. One former colleague, Beverly Malone, recalls Ita routinely showing up around 5:00 p.m. at her office door: "Now?" came the question from behind a cloud of Kent cigarette smoke. And now it was, as they went downstairs to the Parker House for an hour of smokes and scotch and food and gab before returning to work.

Happy memories pour out of Ita's friends even today. In fact, no one seems to be able to speak about Ita Ford without smiling. Most recall her as shy, but with something to say—a "true renaissance woman"—and not incidentally the smartest woman any of the men had ever met. She was a delight at a party, and always delighted to be there.

It was a time in New York history when a slight, brown-haired, left-handed, 26-year-old woman could drink Dewar's and water, and smoke a pack or two a day, and be happy doing what she was doing without burrowing along a career path. She socialized, she took courses at Hunter College, and she enjoyed New York. Eventually Ita moved from her parents' Brooklyn home to wonderful New York, New York, to an apartment close to Greenwich Village, in Sheridan Square.

Still at Sadlier, Ita became a trusted editor, first working on a twelve-volume high school literature program called "Structure in Language and Literature," then as an editor of religious texts, and involved in the earliest Sadlier audio-visual productions. Her co-workers recall her lively cynicism and friendly liberal attitude; she was politically informed, somewhat politically active, and non-partisan in her politics. Dead set like the others against the war in Vietnam, she still did not attend a huge peace rally at City Hall Park.

Ita's reactions to political questions were predictably unpredictable. A California priest-author and friend recalled sightseeing in New York with her: "Ita had a critical mind, non-ideological; even in the mid-sixties we met a fellow taking signatures to stop the building of a nuclear power plant, and Ita challenged the guy to tell us where New York would get power if they didn't build the plant. She said she would think it over before she signed."

As months stretched into years, Maryknoll faded, but she kept up a lively correspondence with her former sisters, now around the world.

VI.

Meeting up in New York with her Maryknoll friends was easier after Ita moved into the two-bedroom apartment in Sheridan Square. Soon her roommate was her high school and college friend Kathy Monahan, and they did what young women did in New York City in 1970, and had a wonderful time of it.

Kathy Monahan recalls living with Ita: she was an incredibly healthy eater ("peas? fish?"), she enjoyed many and varied friendships, and she spent long, long hours keeping up a voluminous correspondence with Maryknollers. In retrospect, although she was away, Maryknoll never really left Ita, and her extended community of friends circled the globe. Neither did she ever decide that marriage was for her. As her relationship with the lawyer ended, she continued to go out with her college crowd, which increasingly included husbands.

There were trips with Kathy Monahan and Anna Mammana: to Provincetown, where they sat on the rocks and talked away half the night; to California and Disneyland, where the ticket seller offered Anna a reduced ticket for her "child"; to Mexico, where they stayed in cheap places and climbed the wall of a fancy hotel to swim in the pool. Letters from Ita's father, words woven into a bright tapestry of memories and presence, arrived at the local Hilton each stop along the way. She shared them, she kept them, she had them in El Salvador the night she died.

Words were important, and Ita was deliberate with them. Her own careful writing belied the fact that it took some time for her to be as precise in speech. She did not speak much in a group, but when she spoke, it was either the funniest or the deepest comment the whole night long.

She also kept her own counsel, and when she announced in 1971 that she was returning to Maryknoll, her friends were both surprised and half expecting it. Ita was not looking for a spectacular life. She simply wished to live and work as a missionary among the poor.

Harry Gaffney recalls her appearing in his office door one day at Sadlier: "I'm leaving," she said. He rushed to counter any offer the competition could have made, but there was no contest. "Maryknoll finally accepted me," she said.

VII.

First she went to St. Louis.

She wrote to a friend: "In the area in which we live, which in my yet not-too-clear sense of direction seems kind of in the middle of the city, I get a strange feeling of one-time opulence. The houses are large stone, three-storey affairs, fit for comfortable burghers at the beginning of the century. Some have turrets and others interesting architectural features. Now I'm sure they are subdivided into apartments, but from the street, you still get a sense of stability, roots, large families, etc."

She was ten years older and ten pounds lighter when she went to Missouri for her second Maryknoll novitiate. Since she had already completed a "canonical year," after seven months or so she was invited to temporary profession as a Maryknoll Sister. On April 29, 1972 she publicly made a Promise of Fidelity "to live poverty, obedience and celibate love in community, according to the gospel counsels and the constitutions of the Maryknoll Sisters until the time of my final commitment." Her Topsfield novice mistress, Sister Paul Miriam, attended the ceremony.

Whatever was left open eight years before was now definitively closed; with the help of God and Maryknoll she had regained her sense of self: "...if we can be ourselves & accept ourselves...obviously limited, weak, imperfect—& accept the mysterious fact that we are loveable—not in spite of ourselves but as we are....You can be

19

who you are—and become more. I know this is true because it happened to me. Who I am now is due to many people who cared for me and those who do now." Her St. Louis novice mistress recalls her as "so ordinary, you'd miss her." She fit in that perfectly.

While at St. Louis Ita gained new friends whose current insights to her personality mirror those with longer knowledge of her: all who knew Ita on a personal level saw that she had suffered deeply in her life. It was not easy for her to leave Maryknoll, and it was not easy for her to decide to go back. One sister remembers: "She was intense, intelligent and extremely sensitive—and her search was to find meaning in her life—to live a life that made sense—and she found it with Maryknoll."

From St. Louis Ita headed toward language studies in Bolivia, attempting stops along the way to visit with other Maryknoll Sisters. "Of course, most of the travel depends on the weather. It will be the rainy season—during which roads, bridges, etc. often disappear in mudslides or become impassible—so we'll see." She eventually made her way to the Institute de Idomas at Cochabamba, Bolivia to learn Spanish—a task both arduous and hilarious, and which also introduced her first-hand to the ingenious ways missionaries have of passing mail along to friends and families. She inquired about one package, explaining its circuitous routing back to Brooklyn: "Down here you'd think Maryknoll was a competing postal system. No one goes anywhere without mail and packages. We even call it a 'would you mind'."

As the "would you minds" continued, Ita was able to report on her possible assignment in a politically tense Chile:

"I am just back in Santiago after roaming around the central portion of the country for seven weeks during which I was supposedly getting some brief idea of what is going on and how Maryknoll is relating to it. I think what happened was that I just got very confused and tired. What happens next is still somewhat up in the air....I'm to be thinking where I go next for a period of in-service training....Some people say I couldn't have come at a more exciting time while others say this is a terrible introduction. I guess that's indicative of what's going on." As Ita began to see the poverty of the people, she began as well to see the purpose of her presence among them. Soon she settled with other Maryknoll Sisters in one of the many squatters' shantytowns that ring Santiago, first in Poblacion Manuel Rodriguez, then in Poblacion La Bandera. "Home is a small wooden house with three bedrooms and a living-dining-kitchen. Also indoor plumbing. It's comfortable and simple....What we hope to be doing here is building community among ourselves, and establishing relationships with some of the people. Just what form that will take for me I still don't know....Because of the history and tradition of the people, there is not much of an emphasis on sacramentalization or other institutional works. Rather it is the hope of the bishop of the area that through developing relations with the people there will slowly evolve a small base Christian community that reflects and prays together. Worship comes later."

When she explained her life to her friends, she described simple presence: "What am I doing? I amble around the poblacion at a very leisurely rate—and if someone looks receptive, I say hello and try some conversation.

Or I go home visiting for a clinic nearby to check up on the babies who haven't been brought for the monthly control. Or I go to meetings or sit in on some adult education classes—women who never finished 8 years and are now in a gov't program to get finished. I also wait on lines—to get food, kerosene or whatever." Her life was to suffer with the people, with the Church: one day planted weapons were found in a tabernacle, and the military detained the priest and searched the entire area. The bishop denounced the whole event as a sham. Her own life churned in the balance: "The tension between Church and state helps keep us all honest. You have to make decisions, even though they won't be popular and can easily be twisted. So we muddle along." She admitted that the kinds of things the Church chose to do and the kinds of things the Church could do were mere temporary measures, because "the Church cannot, should not, take on responsibilities that belong to organized government."

The Maryknoll Sisters ran a mental health clinic for the women of the area. Chile had eighty psychiatrists for the million or so people the World Health Organization said suffered from neuroses at the time, primarily due to the six-year siege of economically disabling military rule. What moved Ita most deeply was the pain of individuals who together comprised a country of poor sufferers, whom she viewed through the faith she sought to share: "I see Chile deeply experiencing the paschal mystery, with the light of Easter still to come...the cup cannot pass without our drinking it."

VIII.

It is difficult to listen to Ita Ford's taped recollections of life in Chile.

The Chilean rule "disappeared" men whose lives and voices became troublesome and made the job complete by destroying their records: they never existed. The wives of the "disappeared" had two choices: they could complain of what happened and risk economic ostracism, or lie that their scoundrel husbands abandoned them, and so get jobs to feed their children. Relief supplies were so scarce the sisters had to weigh the children who came to them, carrying their spoons (there was no money for utensils); those who had gained normal weight were turned away so others could take their places.

Much of what Ita and the others did—could do—was simply be present to the poor. These poor of Chile had perhaps one meal per day; their children saved their milk rations to share with those at home. Once a man said to Ita: "The Church has changed....Before, we had to go up to the Church. Now it's the Church that comes to us." Finding her place in the sacramental, rite-oriented Church, Ita called her work similar to that of a Protestant pastor: "caring, being concerned about, being involved in the lives" of the people. Her frustration was with "the temporary measures that don't touch the source of the problem. At best, they serve as a means of denouncing a situation of sin and injustice."

While Ita had a careful appreciation of the political situations that led to the suffering of the people around her, she did not readily articulate the solutions in political terms. Her ministry was to those affected, independent of cause or reason, and primarily to aid them in resolving their dilemmas. She wrote of her caring for the women and the children especially: "Working with the poor calls for a great restraint and modesty on all levels so as not to overpower, overcome or take over the situation. It certainly has been a great advantage working in La Bandera...a modest presence. There's no church 'plant'; there's no power structure. There's nothing to protect or defend. Money coming for projects such as the dining rooms is channeled through the deanery or zone to be pooled among the other poblaciones of the area."

It was a Church of the poor for the poor, which she saw as credible. For her, "being with the poor means overcoming our distaste of getting dirty literally and metaphorically: the literal dirt, mud, excrement; caring for and supporting the sinner, the underdog, and unpopular causes; entering into messed-up lives; running the risk of being misunderstood, misinterpreted, of being accused as subversives, etc."

Her modest presence made a distinct difference in many lives.

IX.

Progress is often mere persistence.

After six years in Chile, as life within the poblacion deepened, Ita was asked to return to Maryknoll for a "Reflection Year" in preparation for final vows. She tried to postpone, but came as called in the fall of 1978.

She had a missionary's reaction to the abundance of the United States. She still delighted in the people at parties, but the food piled high troubled her; she walked into a party at Sadlier and remarked she could feed her whole poblacion with that spread. She made the rounds of friends, and each noted a new reticence, a new sensitivity. Her repeated falls and consistent compassion for others combined to instill an even deeper sense of self and of the needs of others, perhaps tempered with a bit of embarrassment at her own frailties.

Missionary life is difficult; it was for her, it is for others. At some point the reality crashes in: there is no limit to what is required. She wrote mid-way through her Reflection Year: "One day at mass here the words of the consecration went booming through me—this is my body given for you. The connection was instantaneous—all those giving their bodies—the possibilities there are for us to give our bodies—it was all made so possible & powerful—Jesus' having given his because he loved."

The connection between what happened to her and the love of God was not always that apparent. "Why?" was the enduring question of her life. She was not all that

25

enthusiastic about a year in New York, after the depth and breadth of her missionary experience in Chile. There were four others who shared her Reflection Year; each was in preparation for final vows and none particularly wanted to be in Ossining. They chose to live in the large Maryknoll Sisters' complex, rather than separate themselves off in a small house together, and found grand friendships within and without their little band.

It did not matter that she wished she were someplace else. Ita could still enjoy life. She loved to dance. She loved a good time. She would often meet another sister in a television lounge late on a Saturday night, and the two would scream laughing at "Saturday Night Live."

Typically clad in blue jeans and a plaid blouse, she made it through the Reflection Year. She bounded toward the door for Memorial Day weekend and a few days in Rhode Island, then to Massachusetts with friends before her return to Chile. The call came back to Maryknoll: there had been an accident and Ita, only Ita, was hurt. Fractured pelvis, damaged knee. Why? The question ricocheted around her head as days turned into weeks and months and still her leg needed strengthening. Why? She weighted her ankle with rocks and exercised in the kitchen of the Sisters' vacation house in Watch Hill, Rhode Island, and spoke of people and their needs in places distant: Chile, Zimbabwe, Mozambique. Why? She needed, she wanted, so much to return to Chile, to the people who had no respite from being poor.

As 1979 turned into 1980, she got back to Chile, and started looking for something to do.

X.

The needs of the Church suffering are often articulated by the Church hierarchical, and 1978–1979 brought multiple fractures to Central and South America. The new call came from Nicaragua, and from El Salvador. Again war, again repression, again so many poor, so many refugees. The Byzantine politics of the region were all the more complicated by American assistance.

While Nicaragua had gained some semblance of peace, El Salvador was a cauldron. Throughout this century, fourteen extended families comprised the oligarchy whose interests were protected by the military they controlled. In the early 1960s political parties began to form, and accusations and deaths continued to boil over until a 1979 coup put Colonel Napolean Duarte in power. San Salvador's Archbishop Oscar Romero called for help: guerrillas from various groups were training and hiding in the three-mile demilitarized zone created to maintain the peace along the Honduras border. Their activities, and the forays of their enemies to extinguish them, created refugees who had to walk south, away from what little they had.

For many, the Salvadoran military and National Guard were indistinguishable from the death squads rooting out supporters of the Revolutionary Democratic Front (FDR), the Farabundo Martí National Liberation Front (FMLN), and other, smaller groups. The American Embassy's political section believed that the death squads were "ad hoc vigilante groups that coalesce according to perceived need" although, the Embassy official wrote, "security force members utilize the guise of the death squad when a potentially embarrassing or odious task needs to be performed."

With these wounds, Salvador became a possibility for Maryknoll missionary effort. Ita wrote to her mother: "…after meetings in different countries, it's now been decided that Nicaragua & Salvador—for different reasons—are both congregational priorities for Latin America. As a person between jobs at this point, I've had to look at that priority & say I'm open to consider it. Right now, there are meetings going on in Salvador to establish priorities & job descriptions….In some ways, there's no difference between the needs of Chile & Salvador—there's plenty of work to be done in both. What even makes Salvador a question is the congregation's seeing that it's very important at this time to support Archbishop Romero…."

Ita responded. If the suffering was caused by one or another political situation, it did not matter. The creation of suffering, the creation of need and want and death by individuals marked sinful situations that needed to be addressed by the Church present. So within a few months— from November, 1979 to April, 1980—Ita Ford traveled from Ossining to Nicaragua, to Chile and back to Nicaragua and, finally, in Easter Week, 1980 by bus through Honduras to El Salvador. Archbishop Romero, murdered a few weeks before while celebrating mass at the Divine Providence Hospital in San Salvador, was already buried; so were thirty people killed at his funeral at the Metropolitan Cathedral he refused to complete, his statement on behalf of the poor who now mourned him.

She knew she was moving into a bad situation, and wrote to her mother: "I have all sorts of reactions—from feeling robbed at not having had the opportunity to know Mons. Romero (we're to work in his diocese), to horror at the paranoia & fear of the right & their brutality, to wonder at the gospel message & the impact for acceptance or rejection that it has on people, to feeling with the poor of Salvador & their loss of someone whom they knew cared for them."

As Ita, and her friend and Maryknoll Sister Carla Piette, prayed about the Salvador they hoped to help save from imploding, prayed for the people whose lives they might salve with Christian charity, they knew that the death of Archbishop Romero signaled their own increasing involvements with the Cross of Christ. Her letter to her mother continued: "But we believe that his death will bear fruit—& it's part of the Christian mystery we celebrate this week—and in that same Christian tradition, we'll go to Salvador."

No matter that she was impelled to Salvador by belief, with hope, and because she loved the people there; she knew she had placed herself at risk. She wrote to her friends: "My timing couldn't be worse, I know—but this is the culmination of a process that started last August when the need was foreseen to reinforce the group there. Actually I'm still reeling from Romero's death—because we were supposed to work with him & in some way I guess I feel that part of my future was robbed."

The palpable disappointment at their arriving too late to work with Archbishop Romero continued in her letters: "In His own time the Lord got me here; although since His ways aren't ours, the journey wasn't all that clear at times." But the disappointment transformed itself into hope once she and Carla began to settle into El Salvador: "However, once getting here and having the chance to meet and talk with a number of people, I feel differently. It's a privilege to come to a Church of martyrs and people with a strong committed faith. Though I'm here only two and a half weeks, I have a very strong conviction that I'm where I should be— though the particulars of the future are not very clear yet."

Her words tumbled out of the spin dryer of Salvador: "...an incredible climate of violence....1102 assassinations....It boggles the mind." She continued, in a postcard to friends: "I've been very impressed with the pastoral agents I've met. Last weekend, I attended a course for rural liturgy leaders 'Celebrators of the Word.' There were 60 men participating, the majority farmers, and their testimonies were right out of the Acts of the Apostles. It's awe-inspiring & humbling to come into a church like this."

One can only wonder what an intelligence officer, American or Salvadoran, would make of that. Sixty male "pastoral agents" sounds like the cast of a thriller movie. Add an American or two, and the mix begins to look like a political brew, a steaming cauldron of insurgency ready to challenge the status quo. Too few intelligence officers understand the non-partisanship of Christianity, the extra-political stance of the Christian in the face of what can only be designated as evil. For Ita Ford, and surely for Carla

Piette and the other American missionaries in Salvador, the recognition was the same: "Historically this is not the ideal time to arrive on the scene—but the Lord got us here for some reason."

Finding work was both hard and easy. The Archdiocese of San Salvador identified the department of Chalatenango, in the north, as a priority for its ministry. Ita, the New Yorker, knew well the compactness of the city; rural Chalatenango was a different challenge. She wrote: "It's still a little difficult for me to get a framework around the rural situation—as you have several small towns and then scattered groupings of houses which make up a parish, as opposed to the concentration of people in a poblacion." Ita and Carla saw and weighed different options, different invitations. Some places were too isolated, some were too conflictive. They finally ended up in the city of Chalatenango, a major marketplace about an hour and three-quarters from San Salvador. The winter of Salvador was approaching, where "it often rains all night and some-times there's a short cloud burst during the day. However, the only time I saw a thermometer, it said 96 degrees—so much for winter." The climate was wearing, the heat was explosive.

Within weeks she wrote to her sister that she was "supersaturated with horror stories and daily body counts....I'm not sure how you get 'acclimated' to a country that has an undeclared civil war going...." She also sent along the news that she and Carla had jobs—as workers of the emergency committee in the vicariate of Chalatenango: "What that means is that the church of San Salvador is facing reality & getting ready to help with food, medicines & refugee centers." The army, she explained, was in continual conflict with the various popular organizations that wanted to form a new government, causing people to be displaced, or flee in fear. American military aid was not offset by humanitarian aid. "I don't think we could have dreamed this job up before we came—but we came to help & this is what we're being asked to do....there's a lot of displaced people & disrupted lives—& that's what we'll be focusing on." It wasn't exactly a war. It was a slow and selective massacre.

Ita Ford knew full well what was going on in this country where there were fifty or one hundred assassinations a day: "It's really a complex situation—if only it were as simple as good guys vs. bad—but it's not. And a lot of groups don't have their act together & aren't in agreement about what to do & when. I think a lot of lives are lost that way."

Six months before she was murdered, Ita wrote passionately about the road before her: "I don't know if it is in spite of, or because of the horror, terror, evil, confusion, lawlessness—but I do know that it is right to be here...to walk in faith one day at a time with the Salvadorans along a road filled with obstacles, detours and sometimes washouts:—this seems to be what it means for us to be in El Salvador." The political horror-show displayed itself in the little town square of Chalatenango. Women would come to the Maryknoll Sisters: their husbands had disappeared. Ita would go to the authorities, quietly, to inquire. Every day, it seemed, with one or another of the women, Ita Ford knocked on an official door to ask a military officer about one more human life.

Reality never left her view: "…it really isn't the historical moment for unknown religious to pop into an area where many people are on the run, scared witless & caught in crossfire of the military, trying to wipe out training centers of the popular organizations." She wrote wryly of "the nightly shootings and the daily hearing tests. 'Did you hear that?' 'Yes.' One night I burst out laughing as well—'Yes, our ears all seem to be ok.'"

XI.

They ended up living within feet of a National Guard Barracks, and their activities were surely interpreted in the worst light. How must it have looked to Salvadoran military? Two North American women drop out of nowhere and suddenly, it would seem, they have established a headquarters for refugees (read "subversives" in the government lexicon). Somewhere in the whorls of American-Salvadoran intrigue the story evolved that Ita and Carla were knowingly running a "safe house," that their prayer and service were a front for political intrigue.

They were politically astute, but they were not political agents parachuted in by the revolutionary forces. Their deepest concerns were the meek and the poor, the women whose husbands had been "disappeared," the children for whom law and order was a rifle butt and a scowl. Their classified documents came from Matthew, Mark, Luke and John. Their classified materiel was rice and beans and mercy. They were not stupid; they recognized evil and they recognized what they were challenging.

So that they could visit the poor in the hills, Ita and Carla managed to obtain a second-hand jeep, which they called "Miss Piggy" in honor of its apparent ability to navigate some of the wetter roads. They had their own visitors as well. One Maryknoll Sister, Peggy Healy, became their "Washington commuter." She recalls sitting one evening in the place in which they lived, surrounded by piled-up sacks of food. Ita turned to her and deadpanned: "We're not going to get shot. We'll get killed by the damned food falling on us."

The quintessential New York attitude could help one survive in Salvador, but Salvador did not go away. The faces of Salvador captured Ita's mind and were engraved in her memory. She was convinced of the innocence of the young, and could not believe they were capable of what the military accused them of.

Once Ita went with a mother to identify the buried body of her son, and she spoke later of how those who buried him preserved his dignity even in death. When he was uncovered, there was a white cloth still protecting his face. She shared this recollection with Maryknoll Sister Madeline Dorsey, with whom she and Carla had lived near the coast in La Libertad from April until early June: how peaceful he seemed, how terrible his end, how dignified his burial.

He was perhaps the same youth she mentioned to her niece: "Yesterday I stood looking down at a 16 year old who had been killed a few hours earlier. I know a lot of kids even younger who are dead. This is a terrible time in El Salvador for youth. A lot of idealism and commitment is getting snuffed out here now."

The Salvadoran winter rains did not slow the deaths. In order to maintain some sense of sanity, to relieve the strain of the brutal realities they sought to salve, Ita and Carla often went to La Libertad, to meet with Madeline Dorsey and others to pray, to share a festive meal (if even at the local McDonald's), perhaps to see a movie. Their

extended community enjoyed a population explosion
when Maryknoll Sister Maura Clarke joined Madeline in
August, bringing the ranks of Maryknoll Sisters in El
Salvador at the time to five.

No one of them had any thought to be anywhere except
in Salvador; each accepted her own situation as a part of the
suffering of the people, and hoped their presence and their
ministry would somehow balm the wounded populace. Ita
never doubted: "Again, it's not a question of should we be
here or not —but what does being in this situation call for in
the way of response. It's trying to order a war situation in
some way so you can keep sane and functioning."

The rains continued, and the fighting wore on. One
afternoon, Ita and Carla were approached by a Salvadoran
military officer from the nearby barracks. A young boy, perhaps sixteen, had been accused of collaborating with the
guerrillas. The officer did not want to put him in the
Salvadoran justice system, because nothing would ever
happen; he did not want to keep him, because perhaps he
might have to kill him; his only choice, he continued, was to
give him to the Church.

Their aging jeep, "Miss Piggy," was pressed into service. Ita and Carla drove the boy and some others apparently
released by the military toward their homes. They crossed
the El Chapote River once, and again, as it wound its way
across their path. On nearly the last of the multiple crossings
the river suddenly burst into an angry swell, overturning the
jeep. Ita recalled later she did not know how she got out,
whether she had been pulled by the men, or pushed by
Carla. She somehow bobbed down the river for two miles,

thinking she would soon meet the Lord, until she grabbed the limb of a tree and pulled herself up, to spend the night in the field naked and alone, exhausted, relentlessly bitten by mosquitoes.

Carla was dead.

Ita selected the readings for the funeral, which she attended. She was nauseous, she was dehydrated, she was feverish, she was moving toward pneumonia. She ended up spending four days in the hospital.

The rushing river that overcame them and silenced one life, and the million mosquitoes left to harvest on the living, are metaphors for Salvador. The dark waves crashing out of the contorted politics of the country simply swallowed resistance and carried it away, either in death or to be chewed to pieces in life.

Ita's family grew apprehensive. She wrote to her mother: "I know this is a very hard time for you. I know that you're concerned and worried about the situation and I don't know really how to alleviate that. I truly believe that I should be here and I can't even tell you why. A couple of weeks ago Carla and I were praying and we both cried because it was so unclear to us why we were here, although we felt strongly we should be. Well, it's now quite clear for Carla, but I still have to keep asking to be shown. I can't tell you not to worry—that would be unnatural—it would be like someone saying to me—don't hurt because Carla died. In fact the last few days have been really hurting ones— probably because the shock of the whole thing—the event and to my system—is wearing off. All I can share with you is that God's palpable presence has never been more real ever since we came to Salvador—He's made a lot of things clear to us—what we should be doing, etc.—and I trust in that and I hope you can too."

She recovered, and she did not leave. Carla was dead and buried in Chalatenango with the poor; Maura Clarke came north from La Libertad to join Ita there.

The movements and the very mobility of the North Americans must have been suspicious to their military neighbors. What was Ita Ford doing boarding a long-distance bus on Saturday, September 13, 1980? She was going on retreat. What was Ita Ford doing flying to Nicaragua on November 24, 1980? She was going to a Maryknoll assembly. What was Ita Ford doing flying back to Salvador on December 2, 1980?

XII.

Numbers can only quantify. Ita reported to the Maryknoll assembly: "From January through October 1980, there have been twenty-eight assassinations of Church personnel, three woundings, twenty-one arrests, four profanations of the Eucharist, forty-one machine-gunnings of Church buildings, fourteen bombs, and thirty-three search and seizures of Church properties." It was Thanksgiving in Nicaragua and the Maryknollers celebrated, commiserated, questioned and prayed. Madeline Dorsey and Teresa Alexander had unsuccessfully tried to coordinate their flight back to El Salvador with that of Maura Clarke and Ita; in fact Madeline had telegraphed Ita in El Salvador with the suggestion.

The mail arrived at the parish house in Chalatenango the morning of December 2, 1980. Father Efrain Lopez received another threat, this time a letter. They had all been harassed before. The military harangued them, used its vehicles to block the church entrance. A little later the sacristan was pulled aside and shown a list of names. The killings, he was told, would begin that very day.

Shortly after 2:00 p.m. on December 2, Ursuline Sister Dorothy Kazel and Jean Donovan parked their white Toyota "Hiace" van in front of the main terminal at El Salvador's international airport. The Lanica flight from Nicaragua arrived at 2:30 p.m., with only Madeline and Teresa aboard. No problem, said Dorothy and Jean, they would gladly return a few hours later for Ita and Maura, who were booked on a COPA flight. Somewhere a radio crackled, enough to be overheard or intercepted: "No, she didn't arrive on this flight; we'll have to wait for the next."

The airport was both busy and tense that day; Salvadoran National Guardsmen were making their presence known. On November 27, six leaders of the Revolutionary Democratic Front (FDR) had been abducted and murdered—the 1993 United Nations Truth Commission blamed Salvadoran security forces—and the funeral was to be held the next day. While awaiting Ita and Maura in the terminal, Dorothy and Jean ran into six Canadian nationals who had arrived for the funeral. Within minutes, the Canadians were stopped at a military checkpoint just outside the airport, but let go.

Sub-Sergeant Luis Antonio Colindres Aleman, a twenty-four year old National Guardsman who earned 650 Colones a month and lived with his twenty-year-old girlfriend in a barrio in Ahuachapan, was in charge of the airport detachment that day. He had been alerted to the first airport visit of Dorothy and Jean; at about 6:00 p.m. he was told they were back again. He ordered five Guardsmen to wear civilian clothes, take their G-3 rifles, their gunbelts, and their ammunition cases and to join him in their unit's green jeep, which they had to jump start. They were, he later testified, going out to get some gas.

This is what seems to have happened. At about 6:30 p.m. Sub-Sergeant Colindres Aleman changed into civilian clothes and ordered five Guardsmen to do the same. With the uniformed Guardsman who had come to the barracks to report the return of Dorothy and Jean, they all rode in the National Guard jeep to the airport checkpoint. There he dropped off the uniformed Guardsman, with orders to stop all traffic except the missionaries' white Toyota van. Outside the airport, near the first toll house of the uncompleted toll road, Sub-Sergeant Colindres Aleman and the five others waited for the white van.

Twenty-five minutes later the white van arrived. They stopped it, interrogated the four women inside, and Sub-Sergeant Colindres Aleman ordered three of the Guardsmen to get into the van, one as driver. The two vehicles—the white van with three Guardsmen and the four women, and the green jeep with Colindres Aleman and two additional Guardsmen—proceeded toward El Rosario la Paz, stopping once to restart the jeep. At the National Guard command post at El Rosario la Paz, they stopped again, leaving the unreliable jeep with one of the five Guardsmen to watch it. Sub-Sergeant Colindres Aleman and now four National Guardsmen crowded into the white van and rode toward Zacatecoluca, then six kilometers on bumpy back roads toward San Pedro Nonualco, then even farther along a small dirt road. Then they stopped.

This is the testimony of National Guardsman Carlos Joaquin Contreras Palacios: "The place was uninhabited; they continued about three blocks; they stopped, and Colindres Aleman ordered the women out of the van, and then they raped them, after which Colindres Aleman ordered the Guardsmen to shoot to kill those four women, which they each did; the declarant noticed that Colindres Aleman's gun misfired, so he does not know if Colindres

Aleman actually shot the women; then Colindres Aleman explained that he had given this order because the women were guerrillas or subversives; after this the deponent and the others drove back in the van to El Rosario la Paz with both the interior lights and the radio on."

They had a replacement vehicle waiting at El Rosario la Paz. They took the white van toward La Libertad and set it afire with gasoline. Sub-Sergeant Colindres Aleman coordinated their transportation.

XIII.

Guadalupe Gomez Alfaro lives in San Francisco Hacienda, Santiago Nonualco. At about 10:30 on a Tuesday night early in December of 1980—he does not know the exact date—Gomez Alfaro heard a vehicle pass directly in front of his house. About ten minutes later he heard gunshots, then the same vehicle (from the sound of the engine) passed again in the opposite direction, toward the city. He heard no voices, no groans, no cries.

At 5:30 the next morning Gomez Alfaro went to milk the cows, and about fifty meters north of his house he saw the bodies of four women. He was afraid, and did not go too near them, but he could see that three were blindfolded, one with flowered cloth. Some clothes were near them. At 6:30 a.m. he passed again, and the bodies were still there. They were buried there at ten that morning; he heard that it was ordered by the Judge, but he does not know who buried them. Only later he heard that these were the four North American nuns.

The villagers had reported the finding of the bodies to the local Militia Commander, Jose Dolores Melendez, and soon after two National Guardsmen and three Civil Guardsmen arrived and ordered those gathered there to dig a grave. As the summer sun rose higher in the sky, the local Justice of the Peace, Juan Santos Ceron, authorized the burials of the four "unknowns."

Early on December 4, the news of the burial reached

the local parish priest, who told the Vicar of the San Vicente diocese, who passed the information along to the American Embassy. Father Paul Schindler, a part of the "Cleveland Team" of missionaries that included Dorothy Kazel and Jean Donovan, had already found the burned-out van on the road toward La Libertad. He suspected they were dead. He, too, learned from the parish priest where they were buried, and he was there that afternoon when United States Ambassador Robert White arrived. At the request of the Ambassador, and with permission of the Justice of the Peace, the women were disinterred. They had been stacked one on top of the other in their narrow grave. Ita, the smallest, was on the bottom.

Three days earlier, at the Maryknoll assembly in Nicaragua, Ita Ford had translated some of Archbishop Romero's words about being poor, about being with the poor; she read her translation at the closing prayer service: "Poverty is a force of liberation….It invites us not to fear persecution because believe me, brothers & sisters, he who is committed to the poor must run the same fate as the poor….And in El Salvador we know what the fate of the poor signifies—to disappear, be tortured, to be captive—& be found dead."

XIV.

Fourteen months earlier the Minister of Defense of El Salvador, General Jose Guillermo Garcia, had made known his negative opinion of the pastoral work of some women religious there. Archbishop Romero replied with an opinion of his own: a public condemnation of the Minister of Defense. It was no secret that the Salvadoran military, from top to bottom, despised the Church, from top to bottom. It was no secret that the National Guardsmen had used their Heckler and Koch 7.62mm G-3 rifles to still the senses of four sensitive women. It was no secret that five ordinary men from five ordinary villages in Salvador raped and murdered four unarmed women.

But somehow all the investigations, all the searching for evidence—for rifles, for fingerprints, for names—just did not seem to progress. Somehow things got slow. Then they got even slower. Despite the fact that President Jimmy Carter shut down the dollar spigot to El Salvador three days after the murders, somehow the Salvadoran military thought its own bureaucracy could stall and defeat the search. Perhaps the Americans would lose interest? Proper procedures can take a very long time in El Salvador.

There were two official Salvadoran investigations: a public government commission and a private National Guard investigation. The public commission was headed by Colonel Roberto Monterrosa, Director of the Armed Forces Studies Center. The private self-investigation by (and of) the Salvadoran National Guard was headed by Major Lizandro Zepeda Velasco, who reported to Colonel Carlos Eugenio Vides Casanova.

Five months after the murders, in April, 1981, the American Embassy identified the murderers and gave the names of all six Guardsmen to Defense Minister Garcia. Soon after, the FBI matched Colindres Aleman's thumbprint to one taken from the burned-out van. Perhaps he touched the van in the airport parking lot, he said. Guardsman Jose Roberto Moreno Canjura's weapon matched an expended shell found at the murder site. No, he said, he had not lost possession of his rifle, and he had nothing to do with the murders.

It was clear by then that justice would be slow in coming to El Salvador. The hydra-headed problem seemed to reduce to two points: First, how could a junior noncommissioned officer take five troops on such a mission without the explicit or implicit orders from those senior in their chain of command? Second, if those senior in the chain of command were complicit in the action, how could they direct or cooperate in an investigation that would ultimately end with themselves?

The same "system" that knew its own corruption and turned a budding guerrilla over to the Church, to Ita Ford, now looked to itself for the truth. Ita's comments had barely reached an American friend when the deaths exploded in the world media: "Salvador is distinct from Chile—more brutal, vengeful and lawless. Chile's repression always tried to have the facade of law; not here. No one bothers with such niceties."

It took a long time. Major Zepeda shared his information with Colonel Monterrossa. Within a few months, the investigations were ready to close, with no findings, despite the fact that each officer knew Colindres Aleman was directly responsible for the murders. One can only assume the problem lay—at least partly—in whoever was indirectly responsible for the murders.

Conclusions are hard to come by in any true bureaucracy. The activities of the families of the murdered women, of the Maryknoll Sisters, of members of the media, of so many others with such real and deep concern were fired by initial charges that they were "gun runners." They weren't just nuns, claimed then UN Ambassador Designate Jeane Kirkpatrick that December; no, indeed, said Secretary of State Alexander Haig the following March, they may have been running a roadblock. They believed what they said, but they were wrong. Disinformation and intelligence are such reflective undertakings that it is often impossible to separate impression from outright lie, especially as either moves up to the next higher official with increasing ratification.

The five National Guardsmen were finally accused of the murders and jailed in the spring of 1983. At that time, then Secretary of State George P. Schultz directed an "independent and high-level review of all the evidence available to the United States government pertaining to the churchwomen's case." New York Judge Harold R. Tyler, Jr. headed the investigation, which produced a 103-page document, "The Churchwomen Murders: A Report to the Secretary of State." The document is a trip into the heart of darkness, a look into "a society that seems to have lost its will to bring to justice those who commit serious crimes against it," a look into a military that "sought to shield from justice even those who commit the most atrocious crimes."

The Tyler Report concluded this: The facts were clear enough to show that Sub-Sergeant Colindres Aleman ordered the four National Guardsmen to rape and murder the four churchwomen. The facts were not clear enough to show that Sub-Sergeant Colindres Aleman acted, as he once claimed, on higher authority. The facts were never clear enough to answer why.

Colonel Monterrosa offered a political explanation to the Tyler Commission. He said that the churchwomen were probably subversives. As such, the military would have preferred them eliminated.

Colonel Carlos Eugenio Vides Casanova was commander of the Salvadoran National Guard in 1980. By the time of the trial, he was General Carlos Eugenio Vides Casanova, Minister of Defense. It is very hard to run an underfinanced military. In November, 1983, the U.S. Congress froze $19.4 million in aid to El Salvador pending (demanding?) accountability for the murders. Six months later the trial of the Guardsmen was held, May 23–24, 1984, before Judge Bernardo Rauda in Zacatecoluca. It ran nineteen hours, all through the steamy Salvadoran night. There was a lot of testimony. There was not much of a defense. At one point a defense attorney said, "If they did it, they did it on orders, because in the National Guard if someone does not obey an order of this type...." His thought melted into the night, unfinished.

At 4:15 a.m. Thursday, May 24, 1983 the following persons were convicted of homicide in the deaths of Ita Ford, 40, Maura Clarke, 49, Dorothy Kazel, 41, and Jean Donovan, 27: Luis Antonio Colindres Aleman, Carlos Joaquin Contreras Palacios, Francisco Orlando Contreras Recinos, Jose Roberto Moreno Canjura, Daniel Canales Ramirez. They were the first members of the military ever so convicted. They were sentenced to thirty years in prison.

They are still there. On November 5, 1988 a political amnesty was called for Salvador. They asked to be released; they were denied. The judge ruled that the murders were not a political crime and not covered by the amnesty.

In March, 1993, the United Nations issued the report of its Truth Commission, which determined that the five had indeed followed higher orders, that the whole event was planned in advance. It argued that Major Zepeda and Colonel Monterrosa and Colonel Vides Casanova each obstructed justice. It argued that the military knew what it was doing all along.

XV.

Sister Grace Myerjack is a member of the Maryknoll Cloister in Ossining, New York; she lives there with other contemplative Maryknoll Sisters. She had lived with Ita in St. Louis; she knew her well during Ita's 1978–1979 "Reflection Year." She was also close to Maura Clarke.

Grace spent the early part of the winter of 1980 in solitude. One night, in the seconds before full sleep enfolded her, she saw in her mind's eye both Ita and Maura. The face of Ita and the face of Maura were fully present to her, and they said one simple word: "Come."

They do not look like they are suffering, she said to herself. Why do they need me?

The memory is quite clear to her. They were not suffering. They were complete, they were full. They were who they were.

It was some days later when she heard.